378.76431
R13t

80088

DATE DUE			

THE
TOWER
AND
THE
DOME

Dedicated with deepest love and affection to my wife, Mildred, and to my daughters, Helen and Lenore: their love and support and confidence in me were a tower of strength during this challenging period of my life.

THE
TOWER
AND
THE
DOME

A FREE UNIVERSITY

VERSUS

POLITICAL CONTROL

by

Homer P. Rainey

Pruett Publishing Company

Boulder, Colorado

378.76431
R13て
80088
Sept/1972

ACKNOWLEDGMENTS

I owe a tremendous debt of gratitude to many individuals, groups, and organizations for the loyalty and support accorded me during my term of office as President of The University of Texas. Their understanding of the issues involved in this conflict was a constant source of encouragement to me. I regret that space will not permit the inclusion of each individual name.

Among those deserving special mention and thanks, are: Major J. R. Parten and the other members of the Board of Regents who elected me; Vice President J. Alton Burdine; Dr. Arthur L. Brandon; the late Bernard De Voto of Harper's Magazine; Dr. Blake Smith, pastor of the University Baptist Church of Austin; Dr. Ralph Himstead of the A.A.U.P.; the faculty and students of The University of Texas; John McCurdy, Executive Secretary of the Ex-Students' Association; W. H. Francis, President of the Ex-Students' Council, and all of the members of that Council; Homer Garrison, Director of the Department of Public Safety of Texas; Robert Lee Bobbitt; the late J. Frank Dobie and Dr. Walter Prescott Webb; Dr. Robert L. Sutherland; Miss Ima Hogg; George Sealy of the Sealy Foundation of Galveston; the editors of many Texas newspapers of the day, and numerous educators and educational associations across the country. Finally, I extend thanks to the citizens throughout the state of Texas and especially the citizens of Austin as well as the hundreds of students and ex-students in the armed forces of the nation at the time. To all of these and the others who assisted me in any way, my deepest thanks.

Homer Price Rainey
Boulder, Colorado 1971

CONTENTS

Introduction *1*

The University Begins a New Era *15*

Some Requirements for a First Class University *31*

The Issues in the Controversy as I Saw Them *37*

Reactions to My Charges *55*

My Rebuttal *79*

The Reaction of the Press: Statewide and National *109*

The New Regime—A Tragic Era *125*

Epilogue *149*

INTRODUCTION This is a personal account of a conflict to maintain the ideals of a university against the efforts of a ruling political group to subvert it to their own purposes. The passage of time has not diminished the conflict nor minimized its importance in the development of higher education.

I have waited a rather long time to write this story; I am now viewing it with a perspective of twenty-seven years. This has some very definite advantages. Of course, time does not change the facts, but it does enable us better to understand and interpret those facts in the light of their influence upon later events. It helps us to evaluate the validity of the actions and decisions that were made in the heat of controversy. The decisions that were made then have had profound and far-reaching effects upon the University of Texas and upon all higher education throughout the nation. There is hardly a major college or university in the nation that has not faced issues similar to those encountered in this controversy at The University of Texas.

The reason for the long delay in presenting this story was a desire and hope that an historian would write it. It was such a vitally personal experience for me that I felt it would be better for someone other than myself to do it. I approached several men with the hope that they would write it, but in each case the answer came back that I should do it myself, and that the personal factor in it was precisely that which would give it appropriate perspective—that readers would like to know what this meant to me and how I prepared myself spiritually to deal with a controversy of this nature and magnitude. It is of course, a severe test of one's ideals and courage to stand for them against powerful forces—forces against which one has no legal power, but only the power that comes from his defense of the ideals of great universities. This power, however, I found to be tremendous, and my reliance upon it was one of the great satisfying experiences of my life.

I offer this account to the public, therefore, in the hope that it will make a worthwhile contribution to the vital problem of relating our great universities more effectively to the society which they serve.

This is not a unique or isolated case in the history of American higher education. It is just one in a long series of such conflicts. It is typical of the problem that we have in the United States of relating universities to society. The problem is an old and difficult one, not yet resolved, nor likely to be resolved soon. Universities are among the oldest institutions in Western culture. Through the centuries they have evolved principles and ideals that, from their tradition, are inviolable. Among these ideals is ultimate loyalty to the discovery and dissemination of truth—freedom of research, teaching, and publication. On the other hand, universities are instruments of society. They are created by society, they derive their support from society, and they serve the needs of society. How, therefore, should they be controlled? How can society control them without taking away their freedom which is dearer to them than anything else? Or, from the universities' point of vision, how can they be *in* society and not *of* it?

No completely satisfactory method of governing or adequately relating universities to society has yet been developed. The problem is particularly acute with universities which are provided by the state and supported by public taxation. They have been created by the people to provide them with special services which they cannot provide for themselves in any other satisfactory way. It does not appear logical that the people should create and support them and not control them in some way, and this in our society means some form of *political* control.

Herein, therefore, lies our problem: political control often runs counter to the ideals of freedom so essential to the proper functioning of universities. Politically oriented board members and others often subject universities to their will, and use them for their own purposes. However, the ideals of great universities are virtually universal, and in this sense not subject to local standards and to the whims of local politicians. The standards of great universities are not determined locally. They are determined by the great universities themselves, wherever they may be located.

There is also a timelessness about great universities, in that they represent timeless values. If, therefore, they are subjected to the demands of a particular political or social regime, and are therefore required to conform to a dominant current philosophy, they are robbed of their essential nature and purpose. In fact, the surest way to injure a great state university is to have it fall victim to a political regime.

This was the essence of my battle at the University of Texas: a group of politicians, referred to by J. Frank Dobie as "native Fascists," deliberately moved in to take control, not only of The University of Texas but of all education in Texas. The major purpose of this book is to describe how this was done and what conflict ensued. I do not wish to burden the reader with excessive detail, but enough must be related to prove the charge. The story would not be complete without setting forth something of the political structure of Texas at that time and the relation of that structure to the control of The University of Texas.

The University of Texas is a constitutional university; that is, it was provided for by the Constitution of Texas and not by legislative statute. It is controlled by a Board of Regents of nine members. These members are appointed by the Governor and confirmed by the Senate. Appointments are made for six-year terms which are staggered in such a way that the terms of one-third, or three Regents, expire every two years.

The Governor is elected for a two-year term; consequently, each time a governor is inaugurated he has the privilege of appointing three Regents. If a governor is elected for a second term, two-thirds of the Board will consist of his appointees, and by this process he can if he desires, secure control of the Board by appointing men committed to his policies. This is one of the undesirable features of the system of control in Texas. It is not only true of The University of Texas but of all the other institutions in Texas, including the State Board of Education, which supervises the entire public school system of Texas. This system provides opportunity for an ambitious political group to take over the educational system of the state. This is precisely what was done by the political regimes beginning with the election of Governor W. Lee "Pass the Biscuits, Pappy" O'Daniel in 1938 and extending through succeeding elections through 1946. The details of this take-over are described in this volume.

In order to comprehend fully what happened in this conflict, it is necessary to understand what makes Texas "tick" politically—to understand the dynamic forces which underlie Texas politics. Briefly, five major dynamic factors are at work. They are:

1. Texas has the greatest variety and abundance of natural resources of any comparable territory in the world. It has more than 50 percent of the nation's oil and gas reserves. It is first in the production of many products essential for industry, such as cotton, wool, mohair, sulphurs, and carbon-black.

2. The industries concerned with these resources want the privilege of developing them—or exploiting them, whichever term best suits one's point of view.

3. The key to this development or exploitation resides in the government of the state. It is the government that passes and administers the laws that make the rules of the game, and the government wants the rules of the game to serve its advantage. The Governor is naturally a key factor in this system because of his political prestige and because of his vast control over the system through his numerous appointments to many boards, commissions, and state agencies. Hence, a major objective of like-minded senators and members of the House of Representatives is also very important. The Texas Senate, composed of 31 members, has for many years been

made up largely of lawyers, and it is quite significant that many of these senators are carried on retainer's fees by various corporations. Questions therefore naturally arise as to whom they represent and whom they serve. This is true of many House members as well.

In addition to the Governor and the members of the Senate and the House of Representatives, there are two other very important political personages in the legislative system in Texas: the Lieutenant Governor, who presides over the Senate, also appoints all the Senate committees and directs bills and proposed legislation to the committees of his choosing. In this way he can influence the course of legislation and often determine what legislation shall be passed. The Speaker of the House of Representatives is in a position similar to that of the Lieutenant Governor. Hence, the economic interests want to make sure that they have men who speak for them in these key positions.

To properly reveal all the intricacies of this governmental system would extend far beyond the limits of this study, but as one who has experienced its operation directly, first as President of the University of Texas and then as a candidate for Governor in 1946, I can assure my readers that it is virtually an air-tight system.

4. The fourth factor in Texas politics is the press and other public information media. Those who control economic interests need a friendly press, radio, television, etc. Hence, those interests often go to unusual and even extreme limits to control those news media for their advantage. The "big press" in Texas—media located in Dallas, Houston, San Antonio, and Fort Worth—plays a big role in determining the way people in Texas think. The Texas Quality Radio Network is made up of four clear-channel radio stations located in these same four cities. It is also significant that three of these radio stations, at the time I was President of The University of Texas, were affiliated in control and operation with a leading newspaper in their respective cities. Thus there was a concentration of control of these important news media. I found this combination of control so inimical to the public interest that in my campaign for Governor in 1946 I took the case to the Federal Communications Commission in Washington. This commission held hearings in Dallas on my charges; the hearings re-

vealed some of the major facts about the combined control and resulted in some important changes in their practices.

5. The fifth factor in Texas politics is the necessity to control education—to control or influence the way people think. Citizens vote, and by their votes they help to shape public policies. Those who want to control public policies, therefore, find it desirable and even necessary to control the way people are educated. Thus, they have a basic interest in what is being taught in the schools, colleges, and universities. They want to make sure that nothing subversive to their interests is being taught, and they want the children of Texas to be exposed to the "correct" ideas.

The techniques for controlling what is taught in the schools are varied. There is control of local school boards; there is pressure upon superintendents, principals, and teachers to conform to certain norms. Textbooks are examined, and control of the Textbook Commission, which selects the texts for all the schools of the state, is sought. Teachers' salaries can be kept as low as possible, and teachers intimidated in many ways—by threatening teachers with investigations, by denying them promotions in rank and salary, by subjecting them to loyalty oaths. Control of the boards of higher education can be sought and obtained.

All of these methods were being used when I was President of The University of Texas. The ruling political group, mentioned earlier, moved in to take over the control of that institution. By that time, most of the system of education in Texas was already subject to their domination. In fact, The University of Texas was the only state institution in Texas that had any semblance of freedom left.

W. Lee O'Daniel was elected Governor for the second time in 1940, which gave him the opportunity of appointing six members to the Board of Regents of the University of Texas. These six constituted two-thirds of the board. It was at this point that major difficulties began.

Between his re-election and his second inauguration in January, 1941, Govrenor O'Daniel met with a small group of his advisors in Houston to make plans for taking over The University of Texas. The course of this meeting was delineated in a Texas Senate investigation following my dismissal in November, 1944. The record shows the names of those present at this meeting and what transpired. Governor O'Daniel is reported in the record to have made a speech to the group in which he told them that the time had arrived for them to take over the control of education in Texas, and *especially* The University of Texas because it was the source of all the "radicalism" in Texas education. He explained that the process was quite simple, since he had the privilege of appointing a majority of all Boards of Control. He invited those at the meeting to advise him of the men who should be appointed to these Boards and he would appoint them. It was as simple as that.

All of this was done, and the various boards that control higher education in Texas and the State Board of Education were thus interlocked with representatives of the major financial interests in Texas. For The University of Texas an extremely trying time had begun.

At the very first meeting of the Board of Regents following the Governor's new appointments, a new member of the Board, Mr. D. F. Strickland, who has been a legislative lobbyist for the Interstate Theaters and other large financial interests, sat across the table from me. He took from his pocket a small card and passed it across the table to me. It contained the names of four full professors of economics, no one of whom had been on The University of Texas faculty less than 15 years. He said, "We want you to fire these men." I replied that I was amazed, and asked him why he wanted these men fired. His reply was that "we don't like what they are teaching." My response to that was, "What does that have to do with the matter? Aren't these honorable men, and have they not a right to teach what they know and believe about the subjects which they teach?" I told him also that there were printed Regents' rules in operation under which the university had been operating for many years; that these rules recognized the principles of academic freedom and tenure, which provided that professors could not be fired in this way; that the rules provided that due process must be observed; that this due process allowed them to have charges preferred against them and the right to a hearing upon these charges; and that they could even have counsel to represent them if they so desired. I told him further that if he wanted to prefer specific charges against these men I would set the machinery in motion to provide for a hearing upon his charges. He refused to do this and insisted that they be fired. My reply was that I could not do this, and furthermore that it should not be done because it would violate some of the most vital and treasured ideals of The University of Texas.

Mr. Strickland countered this decision with an attack upon the tenure system and the principle of academic freedom. He said, "Aren't these rules ours (meaning the Regents), and can't we change them if we desire?" I, of course, had to reply "yes" to both parts of this question. The rules were the Regents' rules, and they could change them. But I warned him that these principles were of long standing, and that they were principles upon which all great universities operated. I told him of the American Association of University Professors and of its principles of tenure that practically all universities accepted. I told him what would be the consequences of running counter to them—that the university would immediately become involved in a controversy with this national organization which could easily lead to the placing of the university upon the "censured" list of this organization, and I explained in great detail what would be the consequences of such action.

All of this created some second thoughts on the part of the Regents. After long discussion it was suggested by someone that, instead of taking direct action and changing the rules themselves, it might be a good idea to submit the whole matter to the Attorney General of Texas and ask him for a ruling on the "constitutionality" of using the rules of the American Association of University Professors. They argued that the Statutes of Texas invested the Regents with full powers to manage the university, and that rules promulgated by an outside association such as that of university professors would be contrary to the Constitution and laws of Texas.

This idea prevailed, and preparation was made to ask the Attorney General for an opinion on this issue.

When this decision was made, I asked the board if it would permit me and the faculty to present a "brief" along with theirs to the Attorney General in which we would set forth the case for the rules including the principles of freedom and tenure. This permission was granted, and I appointed a faculty committee to help me draw up such a statement to be submitted to the Attorney General. Our brief made several points about these rules and the principles upon which they were founded. When the Attorney General submitted his opinion, he upheld our contentions on every point, and by this token rejected the point of view of the Regents. This was a significant decision, for it had the effect of establishing these principles in law. This was a major setback for the Regents. They were thwarted in their desire to have the professors fired, and also in their desire to have the rules declared invalid. This meant that they were forced to take some other approach. Their new approach was one of harassment. They took every occasion that arose to harass me and the faculty, and to make life as unhappy for me as possible.

Every meeting of the Board provided the members numerous opportunities for this harassment. The Board met once each month. Prior to each meeting I sent the members a docket, or agenda, for the meeting. The docket contained my recommendations for the operation of the university, and every item had to be approved by the Board in order to be legal. Often this docket included a hundred or more items requiring approval. I, as president, had no legal authority. All legal powers were invested in the Board; I could only recommend actions and policies for their approval. This situation gave the members of the Board opportunities to take issue with the president and to put him on the spot as often as they desired. The items in these dockets varied from such insignificant matters as the recommendation for a $5.00 per month increase in the salary of a secretary to the most important policies for the operation of the university. All faculty promotions and increases in salary had to have the Board's approval. This requirement gave the Regents opportunities for revenge on faculty members whom they disliked. If they couldn't remove those members, they could see to it that all favors were denied them. If, by chance, the Regents' disfavor fell upon non-tenured personnel, the consequences were extremely unfortunate. The celebrated case in this category was that of three young economics instructors who attended a war rally in Dallas and made some adverse comments about the meeting. The details of this case are set forth later in this report.

There was another situation in which the President was at a serious disadvantage, and often greatly embarrassed. Members of the Board would often confer with members of the faculty and deal directly with them. In this way the members of the Board would pick up petty grievances from disgruntled faculty members and then air them in the Board meetings, especially if these faculty viewpoints disagreed with the recommendations of the president. Another problem was that Board members would urge special treatment for their friends on the faculty or staff.

Such direct dealings between members of the Board and the faculty and staff create one of the most serious obstacles to the successful administration of a university. It is a serious matter when Board members fail to accept and approve the recommendations of the president. It betrays a lack of confidence in their chief executive, and when this mutual confidence between an official board and its chief executive is lost, the situation usually deteriorates very rapidly. Some university administrators have even insisted that whenever an official board rejects and turns down their recommendations, it is an invitation to resign. Every administrator has to decide when that time has come for him.

In my case at The University of Texas I chose a course other than resignation. I could have resigned at a number of points along the way, but I reasoned that, in this case, it was not the proper thing to do. I believe that the Regents were so grossly violating the principles and ideals of a great university that they should be faced with their deficiencies and should be held responsible for their mismanagement of the people's greatest public institution. It would have been easy to wash my hands of it, to walk off and leave the chaos to those who created it. However, I felt that such action would betray all men who had gone before me, men who had worked and fought to establish the principles and ideals of the university. I felt that it was my responsibility to fight to preserve these ideals. I believe also that I owed some responsibility to those who would come after me to help create a situation in which university education could function at its best. I concluded that I owed an obligation to the whole educational profession, and to society itself, to help maintain one of the fundamental freedoms so necessary to a free society.

I assure my readers that this was no easy decision. In fact, I wrestled with it for an extended time. I reasoned with myself that in the long run it didn't matter whether I was president of the university, but that the important thing was the manner in which the university was operated. In this way, I was able to set aside all personal considerations and make decisions in terms of what was best for The University of Texas. This gave me in large measure peace of mind, and I believe it gave me added moral force. It was validation for me of the principle that gives meaning and significance to life: one must attach himself to a cause much bigger than himself and lose himself in working for it. This seems to be one of the best-documented principles in all human history.

Hence, after more than two years of struggling with the Regents, I took the initiative and brought the fight into the open by calling a special meeting of the faculty on October 12, 1944, and reading to them sixteen charges against the Regents. These charges are presented in detail later in this report (see chapter 3). The charges described sixteen cases in which the Regents had violated the principles of academic freedom and other principles of good administrative practices.

The effect of making these charges public was immediate and critical. The press of Texas gave them a great deal of attention. Many editorials were written about the critical situation that had developed at the university. Most of these editorials were friendly to me, and called upon the Regents to answer my charges. The *Dallas Morning News*, for example, pointed out editorially that I had stated my case and now it was the Regents' move. The Regents quickly called a special meeting of the Board to be held in Houston on October 31. It is of significance that Houston was chosen for this meeting place, instead of Austin where the Board regularly met. The faculty and students were virtually unanimous in their support of my stands, and the citizens of Austin to a great extent shared the attitudes of the faculty and students. The Regents were in an uncomfortable position, and they sought the friendliest environment they could find. Houston seemed to offer that friendly environment more, perhaps, than any other place—certainly more so than Austin.

In the meantime, between October 12 and October 31, many things happened. The Regents moved feverishly to develop their strategy and build their case against me. The Ex-Students' Association, which had taken an active part in the controversy, held meetings and passed resolutions aimed at finding a satisfactory plan for reconciling the controversy. Their help was of very great value. They appointed a committee of outstanding alumni of the university to appear before the Regents in Houston. The faculty also took a very active part in attempting to resolve the difficulties. It passed a strong resolution supporting me and my administration of the university, and it, too, appointed a committee to appear before the Regents in Houston. In addition, the student body entered the controversy in a very active and positive way. They, too, passed strong resolutions in my behalf and sent their president to the Houston meeting to represent them.

The American Association of University Professors also actively entered the controversy. The executive director of the Association, who had met with the Regents earlier in the controversy over the tenure rules and the case of the young economics instructors, came to Texas again at this time and met with the Regents to interpret to them the ideals and procedures of the Association. He explained to them in great detail what would be the consequences of their possible actions. Thus, the Regents had fair warning of actions later taken against them.

All of this activity set the stage for an exciting meeting in Houston, a meeting which certainly lived up to expectations. The meeting spanned two days and two nights and culminated in my dismissal about nine o'clock on the night of November 1, 1944. The details of these meetings are related in this report.

However, my dismissal did not end the controversy. In fact, the controversy was intensified in many ways. The Board was not unanimous in its action; the chairman of the Board and one other member voted against dismissal, and the ninth member was absent. It was in effect a hit-and-run affair, since six members of the Board either resigned immediately or indicated that they would resign soon. This created a great problem for the Governor, since he had the responsibility of accepting or rejecting these resignations, and of reorganizing the Board. What took place in the Governor's office during the next few weeks has never been fully made known. Evidently there were many high level conferences and much discussion of political strategy. The final result was the acceptance of three of the resignations and the appointment of three new members. There were many rumors that the Governor persuaded three other members to withdraw their resignations and to remain on the Board. The Governor appointed three new members and the Board was re-organized for its first meeting in January, 1945.

In the meantime, many other events occurred. One of great interest was a student demonstration two days after I was removed from the presidency of the university. It might be said that this was an early manifestation of the student protest concept. An estimated 5,000 students organized a parade in behalf of academic freedom. They secured a casket and draped it in black, with a banner of academic freedom spread over it, and marched silently up Congress Avenue and back to the rotunda of the State Capitol, where they deposited it and left it. Austin citizens said that the city of Austin had never witnessed such an impressive demonstration.

The students also held a tremendous demonstration in the university gymnasium with an estimated 10,000 in attendance. One of the features of this demonstration was an address by Dr. Blake Smith, pastor of the University Baptist Church, in which he castigated the Regents for their "high-handed and unwarranted action and their total disregard for the ideals of the university."

In addition, the students called a strike against going to classes which continued for several days.

The faculty, alumni, and many other groups were also very active during this period. The students called for my reinstatement, and the faculty passed a strong resolution also calling for my reinstatement. This resolution was passed by a 92% roll-call vote of the faculty. The alumni and Ex-Students took similar actions.

Before the new Board met in January hundreds of letters and petitions from numerous groups throughout the country had poured in upon the Regents. It was estimated that there were at least 80 petitions asking for my reinstatement.

Hence, the Governor, the Regents, and the ruling political faction in the state were confronted with a difficult dilemma. Should they give in to all these pressures, or should they stand by their guns and try to ride out the storm? They chose the latter course, and the Governor appointed Dudley Woodward, a Dallas attorney who belonged to the "Establishment," as the new Chairman of the Board of Regents.

The strategy adopted by the Regents to block my reinstatement was to attack me personally and to destroy me if possible. The threat of this was made by one of the Regents the night I was fired. He pulled from his pocket a document and brandished it with a statement: "Brother, we will ruin you and see that you never hold another job in American education." That was all that I saw of the document and I do not know what it contained, but subsequent events proved that they did everything possible to make good on the threat.

THE
UNIVERSITY
BEGINS
A
NEW
ERA

My Dream for the

University of Texas

When Dr. Harry Yandell Benedict, affectionately known to all his friends as "Bennie," died in 1937, the first chapter in the history of The University of Texas came to an end. Dr. Benedict was a fine symbol of this first period in the life of the university. He had been a vital part of it for approximately 40 of the 54 years of its life. He came as a young instructor in mathematics and astronomy, went through all the academic ranks, and became the university's president. At my inauguration, Major J. R. Parten, Chairman of the Board of Regents, said, "Credit for much of the present-day plan of the university should go to the late President Harry Yandell Benedict. It was he who drew up many outlines, who wrote countless papers, and who gave without stint of time or vitality his earnest and brilliant thought to the working program of the university as we know it today."

The need and desire for a university had been in the minds of the leaders of Texas from its early days as a republic. In fact, Mexico's indifference to education was listed in Texas' Declaration of Independence as a legitimate cause for rebellion. The Declaration, adopted on March 2, 1836, reads in part as follows: "It [Mexico] has failed to establish any system of education, although possessed of almost boundless resources, and although it is an axiom in political science that, unless a people are educated and enlightened, it is idle to expect the continuance of civil liberty or the capacity for self-government."

After Texas became a republic a series of steps were taken toward the creation of The University of Texas. Mirabeau B. Lamar, for example, when President of the Republic, stressed the urgent need for an institution of higher learning. As a result of his message to the Third Congress of the Republic in December, 1838, an act was passed creating the first part of the endowment for a university and designating Austin as the site for it. However, the actual creation of the university was delayed for quite a long time because of several factors, such as the adjustments to statehood after Texas' admission into the Union in 1845 and the demoralizing effects of the Civil War.

The matter was taken up again in 1876. The Constitution adopted that year called upon the Legislature to "establish, organize, and provide for the maintenance, support, and direction of a university of the first class, to be located by a vote of the people of this state, and styled 'The University of Texas' for the promotion of literature, the arts and sciences." This same Constitution provided for one million acres of the public domain to become a part of the permanent endowment of the university.

But it was not until March 30, 1881, during the term of Governor Oran M. Roberts, that the Legislature passed an act which brought The University of Texas into a reality and added another one million acres of land as additional endowment. Shortly thereafter the people of Texas approved Austin as the site for the university, and two years later, in the fall of 1883, the doors were opened for the admission of students. The University of Texas was on its way. The people also approved Galveston as the site for the medical school, and it began operations in the fall of 1891.

The early period of The University of Texas was marked by a lack of funds, especially for buildings, and by a rather meager support from the Legislature. The two million acres of land granted for endowment were all in the semi-arid sections of West Texas and the grazing rentals on these lands were very low.

During this first period the university was relatively free from political domination and undue political interference. There was one major political clash with a very popular governor who ridiculed higher education and research, but the university had enough strong friends to win that battle. It had a succession of minor clashes with those who desired to suppress a liberal professor here and there, such as Wolfe, Montgomery, and Ayres, and a religious controversy over modern science and atheism which even involved Dr. Benedict. However, the university successfully weathered these attacks and laid a foundation which supported the traditions of freedom of thought and teaching, in line with the traditions of Thomas Jefferson and the University of Virginia. This tradition was so well established that when the university built the towering library which dominates the campus and can be seen for many miles on the Texas landscape, carved in stone over the main entrance were the great words of religious and political freedom: "Ye shall know the truth and the truth shall make you free."

The university had also incorporated the concept of freedom of thought and teaching into the Regents' rules for the governing of the university which guaranteed these rights to the faculty, and had included a tenure system to protect them.

Hence, academic freedom had been cherished at The University of Texas and had been relatively secure—as secure as it had been in most other state universities, and in Texas the university was the leader for those ideals among all the other colleges and universities. In fact, at the time of the controversy described herein, The University of Texas was the only institution in Texas that had any semblance of academic freedom left—this freedom had already disappeared from Texas A & M and Texas Tech.

Immediately following World War I, there began in Texas an enormous industrial development, built upon the vast natural resources of Texas—principally oil and natural gas, but also upon many other raw products that industry needs, such as sulphur, cotton, wool, mohair, cattle and cattle products. It was clear that Texas had a big industrial future, but for this industrial era Texas had a number of handicaps to overcome, such as lack of industrial capital, discrimination in freight rates, and a shortage of trained scientists and technicians and skilled labor. Texas also had some strong ideological and psychological factors to deal with. The minds of Texans were products of the frontier—a ranching and agricultural economy. Much of Texas, especially the eastern half of the state, belonged to the Old South with its concepts of white supremacy and Greek democracy. Religiously, Texas belonged to the Bible Belt and the extreme fundamental wings of Protestantism. Historically, Texas was politically Democratic, but more in the line of Woodrow Wilson than of Franklin D. Roosevelt. Texas was strongly states' rights, strongly anti-labor, intensely parochial and vocally boastful and proud—emotional, sentimental, and enamored of hot political fights. For a generation the issue of prohibition had provided Texans with a moral issue upon which they could crusade to their hearts' content; Sunday movies and horse racing were of the same order.

Franklin D. Roosevelt's brand of democracy and economics, his labor policies, his attack upon the Supreme Court, his friendliness to the Negro population, and his ideas of a strong government in Washington all threw Texans into confusion and finally into opposition. They were unhappy about Roosevelt's third campaign in 1940, but they went along; however, by 1944 they were ready to pull out and form the Texas Regulars. In 1948 Texas Democrats joined the Dixiecrats, and in 1952 voted for Eisenhower. They had previously bolted the Democratic Party in 1928, primarily over the religious and prohibition issues.

While all this was going on in the economic and political areas, The University of Texas was healthily pursuing its way toward becoming a first-class university. Oil had been discovered on its two million acres in West Texas, and the university was rapidly coming into the money—big money—and there was much more to come, not only from its own lands but also from private wealthy Texans who needed some worthy place to leave their fabulous fortunes. The McDonald Observatory for astronomy provided the university with the finest instrument in operation at that time. The Will Hogg

Foundation for Mental Hygiene was established and was later greatly expanded by the grants from Miss Ima Hogg; the Mike Hogg Foundation for Municipal Research added further facilities to the university. Other private gifts included two from Major Littlefield which meant fine things for the university. One of these was a gift for the purchase of the Wrenn Collection of English Literature. Another was a gift of $125,000 to be used for the writing of a history of the South. From the Stark family of Orange, Texas, came a collection of rare books in English literature.

By the 1940's The University of Texas had been admitted into the Association of American Universities, which was composed of fewer than 40 of the outstanding graduate schools in North America. It and the University of North Carolina, University of Virginia and Duke University were the only southern members of this association. A tremendous campus was under construction. A new school of fine arts had been added, and four bureaus of research, primarily designed to promote research in the natural resources of Texas that would help toward the industrialization of Texas, had been organized. A Latin American Institute was planned to help facilitate our Good Neighbor Policy with Central and Latin America, as the university was on the road to Latin America. In addition there were plans for a university press, a library school, and a school of social work. Teachers' salaries were being raised and a classification of Distinguished Professors had been created.

In a word, The University of Texas was well on its way. Its leaders, among both the administration and faculty and the Board of Regents, knew what a great university should be, and they were determined that they were going to have such a university for Texas.

The university had had several outstanding men as leaders for the Board of Regents; among those were Major Littlefield, Colonel Breckenridge, Mr. Gregory, and Major J. R. Parten. These men all knew that a great university must be kept out of politics as nearly as possible; in fact, they had said that the university should not be in politics at all—that it should not become a political football. Major Parten, for example, often said to political leaders that he would "play politics" with them on anything in Texas except the university. There he drew the line.

These fine Regents had created an excellent tradition for The University of Texas. They had fought its battles against all those who would injure its integrity or who would prevent it from functioning as a university should function.

When President Benedict died in 1937 the leaders in the Board and on the faculty and among the Ex-Students realized that a crucial stage had been reached in the life of The University of Texas. They sensed its outstanding opportunities and potentialities. They knew, too, that the full realization of these possibilities depended upon the quality of its leadership in the period immediately ahead.

Hence, under the leadership of the Board of Regents, the faculty and the Ex-Students' Association were called upon to help search the country to find the right man for the presidency of The University of Texas. Each group appointed a committee from its ranks to work cooperatively on this project.

These committees went about their job in an efficient, intelligent manner. They allowed themselves plenty of time and asked the faculty to complete a list of presidential possibilities. The first such list contained nearly 200 names prominent in American education. The committees then began the long process of evaluation and elimination which occupied nearly two years.

The search ended in December of 1938 with my selection for the presidency of the university. I had met the approval of all three committees, and was recommended by all of them to the Board of Regents.

I have remarked many times that I became President of the university under the most favorable circumstances that one could desire. I had the unanimous support of the Board of Regents, faculty, and Ex-Students. What more could one want? Unhappily, political storm clouds were already appearing upon the horizon.

I saw in the situation an outstanding opportunity to relate the university to the people in such a fundamental way that the welfare of the people would be greatly improved, and the cultural influences of the university could become very extensive in not only the life of Texas but the entire southwestern region.

The interest of the general public was so widespread that, at my inauguration, approximately two thousand people attended various sections of a three-day program, which included, in addition to the inauguration exercises, five major conferences dealing with the state's responsibility toward education. Newspapers and magazines alone printed more than ten thousand inches of copy relating to the different phases of the occasion.

In my inaugural address I attempted to give an answer to a basic question: Why do a democratic people tax themselves to support a system of higher education?

I said that my primary desire is so to interpret the university to the people of Texas that they may appreciate the contribution the institution has made and may continue to make to their well being. Many people look upon an institution of higher learning as something far removed from the activities and needs of their daily lives.

It is my belief that the citizens of a state support a university because they believe it can contribute much to the public welfare and that a society cannot achieve its most desired goals without the aid of such an institution. That faith has been eminently justified in many of the great state universities that have sprung up throughout the nation in the last hundred years. These institutions have been close to the people. They belong to the people. They are controlled democratically and are responsive to the commonweal. This, in my judgment, is their glory and the chief reason for their success. It is worth noting here, also, that they are no less universities for being democratically sponsored. It was commonly thought for a long time that because state universities belonged to the people and were under the control of the political branch of the people's government they could not become true universities, that they could not enjoy proper academic freedom, that they could not further significant research or promote genuine scholarship. We have the word of the president of one of our greatest endowed universities that the state institutions can do, and are doing well, all the things that endowed universities are accomplishing. Private institutions no longer have a monopoly on scholarship, research, good teaching, or even academic freedom. It is a matter of record that most of the breaches of academic freedom, as shown by the cases investigated by the American Association of University Professors, have occurred not in state universities but in private ones. My faith in an educated citizenship leads me to feel that state universities can stay close to the people and serve their needs and yet do these things without surrendering their freedom or the other factors that make them real universities. Furthermore, I believe that it is relatively easy to convince the masses of educated people that freedom is essential to learning and to service of the highest type. The few munificent donors who support endowed institutions do not necessarily possess a keener appreciation of the values of freedom than do the many taxpayers. If a democratic society understands that it needs scholarship, research, good teaching, and an academic freedom that will foster these pursuits, then I believe that intelligent people will provide for these functions in tax-supported institutions.

We want, therefore, to hold this University to the fine tradition of our best state universities and to make of it a scienific, intellectual and cultural center for the life of this great commonwealth.

I asked further, What are the functions of this university?

It is essential to inquire definitely what such a commitment entails. The present state of life in Texas and the world demands that we make a fundamental inventory of our social institutions. Universally, social and political organizations are being scrutinized today, individual and collective ideas are being scanned, and common practices investigated in an effort to discover the weaknesses of contemporary society and to correct them. This seems an appropriate occasion for examining and inquiring into the fundamental functions of state universities and of The University of Texas in particular. Such we have tried to do in the conferences which have preceded this inauguration. The purpose of my address today is simply to declare that the furthering of the functions, obligations, and responsibilities identified by the speakers in these conferences will become the major objectives of my administration.

Some of the conclusions of these conferences, therefore, I wish to present. I cannot, of course, discuss all of them, nor would it be appropriate to do so. But it is my desire to lay special emphasis upon a few of them.

I should like to direct your attention, in the first place, to the fact that in the building of a great commonwealth certain geographic, social and economic factors are of essential significance. These are: first, the *natural* resources of a region, such as soil, climate, and minerals; second, the *human* resources, such as the types and quality of the people; and third, the *cultural* resources, such as its history, traditions, and folklore. The effective development of these resources depends largely on science and education and the maintenance of our free social and political institutions. This significant fact is the first major conclusion of our conferences.

A second conclusion of these conferences is that a university has a distinctive role to play in the development of a state—a two-fold obligation, if you will—namely, to aid the people of the state in the determination of their social goals, and to develop the techniques and provide the intellectual leadership necessary for the achievement of these goals.

Viewed in this way these functions place the university at the very heart and center of our social institutions and identify it as perhaps the most fundamental agent in our cultural evolution. There are many, perhaps, who will quarrel with this conception of a state university. There are some who even seriously question whether we can use modern science for the determination of social goals. I am willing to admit that we are now achieving only a fraction of the benefits of science for this purpose, but it would seem to me to be a denial of the primary function of intelligence to argue that the results of science and invention cannot be used in determining social goals. It would also be a denial of the highest gift of human intelligence; namely, the ability to think creatively.

If our learning and experience cannot help to lead society toward better ends it is indeed a dark prospect.

There are others who, granting the ability of a university to aid in social betterment, take the position, however, that such an institution should not participate actively in this process. This opinion, in my judgment, is untenable, and furthermore is one of the serious defects in much of our educational philosophy. It has become quite the habit in recent years for scholars and scientists to disclaim any social or moral responsibility for the results of their research. It is however, a hopeful sign that both the British Academy of Science and the American Association for the Advancement of Science, in their respective conventions in the last three years, have acknowledged publicly the social obligations of science. There are tremendous contributions which this University can make to the life of the state if we take this view of its office and avail ourselves of the opportunities that are presented to us.

The third emphasis of our conferences, in fact, was upon those opportunities which seem to belong peculiarly to The University of Texas and which, wisely developed, would redound to the good of the state.

This, then, was a statement of my dream for The University of Texas.

At the beginning of my administration, The University of Texas was just beginning to make its bid to become one of the truly great universities in the country. Up to this point it had been a young institution. It was a full generation or more behind some of the great state universities of the Middle West. It was just getting into a position where it could make great strides.

Until recently it had suffered in competition with the other universities of the country in maintaining an outstanding faculty simply because it didn't have the money to attract them and then hold the highly qualified. If the university could have brought back to its faculty the members that it had lost since 1920, it would have had one of the outstanding faculties in the nation. These men were now leading scholars in other institutions. The university had, therefore, been drained of its best minds for a long time. It was in effect a training ground for other universities.

By 1944 that tide had been stopped. During the period from 1939 to 1944 we were proud of the fact that we had not lost a single faculty member that we had desired to keep. We were getting to a point where we were able to compete with other universities for good personnel in terms of salaries, what we could offer for research, and other advantages. Without disparaging any other southern institution it could be said that The University of Texas was not in close competition with a single institution in the South; there was not a university in the South that could pull faculty members away from The University of Texas. In fact, the trend was the other way, and The University of Texas was beginning to compete with institutions like Michigan, Minnesota, California, Chicago, and Harvard in excellence of both faculty and facilities.

The arrangement for optimal use of the university's observatory is illustrative. In the spring of 1939 The University of Texas had dedicated the McDonald Astronomical Observatory in the Davis Mountains in southwestern Texas. The observatory was the gift of Mr. McDonald of Paris, Texas, and contained an eighty-two-inch reflector. At that time it was the second largest mirror in operation, and was regarded as the finest instrument of its class in existence. However, The University of Texas did not have the personnel to staff it. The University of Chicago was in just the opposite condition. It had an excellent astronomy faculty, but it needed a new observatory. Such a situation provided an excellent opportunity for inter-university cooperation, and an agreement was reached by which The University of Texas would provide the observatory and maintain it for a period of thirty years, and the University of Chicago would furnish the staff, with the research results to be published jointly. This proved to be a highly successful arrangement, and possession of the observatory had at once placed The University of Texas along with the University of Chicago in the front ranks of astronomical investigation.

The case of Dr. Ernest Lawrence, atomic physicist of the University of California, illustrates the university's competition for outstanding faculty. At this time atomic physics was holding the center of interest in the physical sciences and everybody was discussing the cyclotron and the smashing of atoms. The man who seemed to be the leader in this important new area was Dr. Lawrence. He had a cyclotron of limited power, and he desired to build a much larger and far more powerful instrument. However, such an instrument was very expensive; it was estimated that it would cost at least $750,000 to construct. Dr. Lawrence had tried for some time to secure the necessary funds from his own university and from some of the foundations, but he had been unsuccessful, and he was restless and champing at the bit. He was stymied.

I learned of this situation and began to explore it. I reasoned that if we could capture Dr. Lawrence and build a big cyclotron at The University of Texas we would gain leadership in this field as we had in astronomy with the McDonald Observatory. Most fortunately, The University of Texas had over one million dollars of idle funds that could be used for this or any other good purpose.

I discussed this situation with members of the Board of Regents, and they encouraged me to go see Dr. Lawrence and talk the situation over with him. I flew to Berkeley and had a personal interview with Dr. Lawrence, and I learned that he and his colleagues were on the verge of making startling new discoveries in the release of atomic energy, but that they were being held back for want of an adequate cyclotron. When asked if he would be interested in coming to The University of Texas, he replied that he would be interested on one condition, namely, if The University of Texas would build a big cyclotron. Upon being told that there were enough funds in the bank to build it, he immediately became enthusiastic and said that if The University of Texas would build the cyclotron, he would come and bring his whole staff with him. This looked good both for him and for The University of Texas. It looked as if the man and the institution had found each other.

Subsequently Dr. Lawrence made a trip to Austin to look the situation over first hand. While in Austin he met with the President and a committee of three of the Board of Regents and discussed the matter at great length. The Regents committee, too, very enthusiastic about the possibilities of bringing Dr. Lawrence to The University of Texas and of building the big cyclotron and of stepping into the lead among American universities in atomic research. It looked like we were all set and ready to go. However, Dr. Lawrence said that he would have to give the University of California another chance to see if it could raise the funds to build the big cyclotron.

When the people in California saw there was a possibility of losing Dr. Lawrence and his staff they went into action to try to raise the funds. They tried sources in California and they tried elsewhere. They appealed to one of the large educational foundations in New York and reportedly were told that this foundation could not enter into competition between the University of California and The University of Texas and that that situation would have to be resolved before it could act upon such a request.

This seemed to produce a temporary stalemate; California could not raise the necessary funds, and the foundation could not take part at that stage of developments. Meantime, The University of Texas was necessarily awaiting developments. After a period of time in which it seemed that the University of California had exhausted its possibilities, it looked as if atomic research would come to The University of Texas. When the project came back to the Board of Regents in this form it had the enthusiastic recommendation of the President and the Regents committee, and quick approval was anticipated. When the plans were presented to the entire Board, however, there appeared to be considerable timidity and reticence on the part of two or three members. It was a big project, and they didn't understand atomic power at that stage and failed to appreciate its possibilities. Furthermore, they were afraid that the Board might run into political repercussions with the Legislature if such a large sum of money were spent on something so new and experimental as a big cyclotron. Hence, they urged caution, and wanted me to explore the possibilities of getting a foundation to share the expense with The University of Texas. Well, the University of California had first call upon the foundations, so this door was virtually closed to The University of Texas. The result was that we were not able to secure unanimous and hearty approval of the Board of Regents, and thus the matter had to be dropped and The University of Texas lost its magnificent opportunity to seize the lead in atomic research. World War II was just around the corner, and the atomic age was less than five years away.

Just as soon as it appeared that The University of Texas would not go ahead with the building of the big cyclotron the Rockefeller Foundation made a grant of $1,250,000 to the University of California for its construction, and the University of California became the leader in the field of atomic research instead of The University of Texas.

This was a tremendous disappointment to me and to some of the Regents as well. In looking back over the negotiations it can be seen where we failed for The University of Texas.

If, when Dr. Lawrence came to Austin and met with me and the Board committee of three, he had met with the entire Board I believe that he would have sold the project to the whole Board as he had done to me and the committee. This was a technical mistake, but it was a natural one in the circumstances. The Board had already discussed the project favorably and had appointed the special committee to explore the matter. It never occurred to anyone that a favorable and enthusiastic recommendation by the President and this committee would not be sufficient.

It is almost certain that if the Regents had promised to build the big cyclotron The University of Texas could have secured help from the Rockefeller Foundation—help which went to the University of California just as soon as it was decided where Dr. Lawrence was going to work. Such are the turns of fate and fortune!

This case provides an excellent example of how Regents who are politically minded and who do not know what a great university should be doing can hold a university back and doom it to mediocrity or something less than its best. Their political-mindedness caused them to hand the medical school of the university a similar fate (see Chapter 3, point 16).

In my inaugural address I also raised this question: What is the function of a state university? I answered it by saying that one of the major objectives of the new administration was to define the basic relationship between a people and their state university. We tried to find a functional answer to the question of why the people of Texas tax themselves to support a great university; what do they expect to get out of it that they wouldn't get from another type of educational system? The answer to this question is found in the following reasoning: it couldn't be successfully argued that The University of Texas was essential or indispensable to the life of the state or to the being of the state, because the state existed before it had a university, and it would continue, after a fashion, if the university were closed. But on the other hand, when a democratic people set out to improve their well-being, to raise their standards of living, and to enrich their lives, it is likely that they have never devised an instrumentality that is potentially as great a servant for them as a great university. That was my conception of the real function of The University of Texas in relation to the people of the state who supported it. It is their servant. It is potentially one of their greatest assets.

It can be argued with considerable success that the wealth of a state is dependent upon three major factors: (1) its natural resources, (2) the native ability of the people, and (3) its education in terms of training and skill and social and governmental organizations.

When this formula is applied to Texas, one gets some significant results. In terms of natural wealth, Texas has the greatest abundance and variety of natural resources of any comparable piece of territory in the world. In terms of the second factor, it is likely that the native ability of Texans will compare favorably with other people.

These two factors—natural resources and native ability of the people—are fairly constant; that is, they don't change much over a period of time. Those natural resources have been here for thousands of years, but they have had to wait for the development of modern science and technology before they could be useful. In a very fundamental sense a resource is not a resource until it is available for use. It is, therefore, only the third factor of education and social organization that is variable. To the extent that this is true it may be argued that a people's wealth and well-being vary directly with it.

What is the record of the relationship between these factors in Texas? Texas ranked thirty-eighth among the states in education in 1940—tenth from the bottom. Texas and the South generally strenuously resisted scientific and technological training for a hundred years. They offered practically none of these types of training until quite recently. From 1883, when The University of Texas was organized, to 1916, it did not give a single graduate degree in any of the branches of engineering—mechanical, electrical, chemical or petroleum; all of these fields of technology were completely neglected. Prior to 1916 it gave only six graduate degrees in physics, and only twenty-three in chemistry.

Texas was just beginning in any real sense to develop a program of scientific and technological training that could make use of its great storehouse of natural resources. Prior to this time Texans who wanted such types of training had to go to northern and eastern universities to get them, and records show that a vast majority of those who left Texas to get their training never returned to Texas. When a large pulp and paper mill was built in East Texas, there was not a single technologist in Texas that could be hired for that plant. Every one of them had to be imported into Texas from the outside.

This, too, influenced my conception of what The University of Texas should be doing for the life of the state; the university ought to be training these scientists and technicians. When a university is thought of in these terms it is not a luxury. It is the greatest economic asset that a people have— all over and beyond the cultural, moral and spiritual values of such an institution.

It was a major objective of my administration to develop this kind of a functional program for the people of Texas at their university.

Closely coupled with this functional idea was another very important one. It was believed that The University of Texas had never fully lived up to its opportunity to sell itself to the people—to interpret itself to them as their university to improve their well-being and to enrich their lives. For a generation there had been a political influence in the state that was hostile to higher education, an influence which had ridiculed higher education and research and taught the masses of the people to think of higher education as something of a highbrow country club for boys and girls of rich parents, using the people's money for research and experimentation on white rats, and all that kind of business. The people of Texas needed a new concept of their university. They needed to understand it.

To give this to the people of Texas I set out to develop a good department of public relations. This policy was in line with the recommendations of a special faculty committee which had made a long and careful study of the university's needs for such a department. The policy was also approved by the Board of Regents and I was promised by the Board as one of the conditions of my appointment that I could select and bring with me a man well qualified in this field.

For this purpose Dr. Arthur L. Brandon was employed. He was well known to the President, and was recognized as a leader in this work. His work at The University of Texas was very successful. This was reflected in many ways, but primarily in the pride the people of Texas have in their university. In fact, the university became the chief object of their pride. This was reflected in the fact that the university's enrollment held up better than that of any major university during World War II. It was also reflected in a more favorable attitude of the Legislature and greatly increased appropriations.

This, then, was the program and the ideals of my administration. It soon became apparent that these ideals were in conflict with the dominant group on the Board. The chapters which follow are a consideration of the details of these differences.

This controversy was fundamentally a clash between two systems of thought—two ways of life. It was a clash between a dominant business culture on the one hand and Judaeo-Christian ethics on the other; between reactionary *nouveau riche* capitalism and the concepts of a liberal democracy; between the Old South and the New; between the ideals of the frontier and modern industrialism; in a word, it was the conflict between the old world and the modern world.

I have described these issues as seen by myself and by other groups such as the faculty, the ex-students, the students, the Board of Regents, and finally the state and national press.

I have also presented the results of the investigation made by the American Association of University Professors (A.A.U.P.), the Southern Association of Secondary Schools and Colleges, and the National Chapter of Phi Beta Kappa.

In order that these issues may be presented as authentically as possible, I have drawn heavily upon the original documents, and have quoted extensively from the records of the Texas Senate's investigation of the controversy, made immediately following my dismissal in November of 1944. I have tried to give all parties to the controversy the opportunity to speak for themselves in their own way.

SOME REQUIREMENTS FOR A FIRST CLASS UNIVERSITY

Thus, my administration of the university was launched under very fortunate circumstances, and upon the ideals and objectives outlined in the preceding chapter. I was filled with enthusiasm, and was eager to undertake the realization of these great potentials of the university.

In order to realize these goals and to develop the university into an institution of the first class as required by the Constitution of Texas, there were several significant requirements that must be met.

In the first place there is needed a clear definition of the purposes of the university in (1) the system of higher education in the nation; (2) the system of education in the state in relation to the public schools, the junior colleges, and the other units of the state educational system; and (3) developing the natural, human and cultural resources of the state.

It was a major purpose of my administration to spell out these functions in concrete terms, and to develop a program of action for their realization. This required the understanding and help of the Board of Regents and the faculty, and the sympathetic help of the people of Texas expressed primarily through the support of the Legislature. This task involved both immediate and long-range programs.

We worked closely with the educational leaders of the state in developing these relationships. For example, I called together the leading junior college people and asked them how the university could be of greatest help to junior college education in Texas. They made one very concrete proposal: we should seek the finest junior college educator in the nation and put him on our faculty to work with junior college leaders throughout the state and help in every way to promote junior college education. When I asked these leaders to suggest the man that they thought would best fill this position, they recommended Dr. C. C. Colvert, then in Louisiana. He was employed and is still on the faculty. Under his leadership The University of Texas has for all of these years held a commanding leadership in the field of junior college education, and Texas has an outstanding system of junior colleges.

In the second place, problems relating to the faculty are central to the development of a university of the first class. A great faculty is the heart of a great university. I have often thought that in this connection an administrator has primarily two major responsibilities: (1) to select and recruit the best faculty that he can find within the limits of the institution's financial resources, and (2) to create for the faculty the best possible conditions for the doing of their work. It is the faculty who give quality to the institution, and that is by far its most important educational asset. Once the faculty selection process has been carefully worked out, the next important matter is the development of sound personnel policies. These personnel policies determine the morale of the staff, and it is this intangible thing—morale, arising from the attitude and feeling of those who do the work—that conditions the effectiveness with which the objectives of an institution are realized.

It was in the area of faculty personnel policies that I encountered some of my most difficult problems with the Board of Regents. Some of these problems are detailed later in this report, but it might be pointed out here that the most basic factor in this problem arose out of the differing attitudes of the Board of Regents and of the faculty toward the faculty's relation to the administration. The members of the Board tended to look upon the faculty as employees and upon themselves as employers. If there is any one thing that will cause faculty members to get their backs up, it is to suggest that they are employees in the modern sense of industrial workers. This attitude of the Board expressed itself in a number of ways, but especially in their attitudes toward faculty tenure and academic freedom. Certain members of the Board referred to the A.A.U.P., which was organized for the protection of faculty freedom and tenure, as the professors' "C.I.O. labor union." These Board members represented the attitudes of the modern industrial system, and this was both the harshest criticism that they could make against the faculty and the one most resented by the professors. In the long tradition of universities in the western world, faculty control of major university policies has been a chief characteristic of their administration, and, as was indicated earlier in this report, The University of Texas from its beginning had had the strongest element of faculty control of any major university in the nation. Thus, the strong contrast between the attitudes of the Regents and the faculty on this matter of control was the chief item in the controversy of my administration of the university. If a university is to be a true university, it cannot surrender its freedom to anyone. Nevertheless a political group deliberately planned to take control of all education in Texas, and especially of The University of Texas, because, as Governor O'Daniel had said, the university was the source of much of the "radicalism" in Texas at that time. In other words, the university must become an instrument in a political group's control of the thought and life of the state.

It goes without arguing that a university cannot become great without adequate financial support. Everything depends upon this factor. From its origin The University of Texas has been committed to the furnishing of free, higher education to the youth of Texas. The Constitution of Texas not only demands "a university of the first class," but also provides that no tuition should be charged the students. This is one of the greatest commitments that any people have ever made to its youth, and the people of Texas have charged their legislature with the responsibility of providing the funds necessary to the fulfillment of this commitment. The earliest constitution of Texas set aside millions of acres of land to serve as a permanent endowment for the university and the public schools of Texas. The result of this farsightedness has been that The University of Texas now has one of the three or four largest endowments of all the universities in the nation, and also one of the largest permanent public school funds in the nation. These land endowments are famous throughout the nation, and are the bases of Texas' support for free education for all its youth from the kindergarten through the university. However, because these funds have been so significant, there has been a strong tendency for the Legislature to depend upon them to the extent of failing to make adequate supplementary appropriations to meet the needs of the public schools and the system of higher education. The result of this failure on the part of the Legislature to provide adequate funds is that Texas' educational program for many years ranked among the lowest in the nation.

The university, too, suffered from this neglect on the part of the Legislature. For example, in 1920 the Legislature provided through appropriations 80 percent of the total educational expenditures on the university. In 1925 this percentage had increased to 85.7 percent. But since 1925 this percentage has been very materially reduced, and during the fiscal year 1943-1944 had declined to 57.8 percent. With this reduction in proportionate legislative support, the university had to depend more and more upon local funds and gifts and grants to ensure an adequate program. Naturally, therefore, greater support from the Legislature became one of my prime objectives. I knew, first of all, that Texas was abundantly financially able to provide for a first-class educational program. The problem was simply a matter of providing an adequate and equitable system of taxation to provide the needed funds. It was perfectly clear that the great natural resources and the industrial system of Texas were not bearing their just share of these needed funds. The business and industrial leaders of Texas had for many years controlled the governmental and legislative structures of the state to such an extent that practically all appropriations for education were subject to their control. The legislative halls swarmed with their lobbyists to help prevent any "undesirable" legislation. The ultimate of this control of education was the placing of their representatives on the boards of control of the schools and colleges and universities of the state. Under the administration of Governor O'Daniel this control became virtually complete. During my first legislative session, when I appeared before legislative committees seeking additional funds for the university, I found the lobbyists for these interests sitting on the *opposite* side of the table seeking to prevent increased taxation. I accepted this as a fair fight. But then Governor O'Daniel placed some of these same lobbyists on the Board of Regents, and I found that they were now on my side of the table, and trying to prevent our asking for increased appropriations. This, I thought, was unfair, and it placed me and the university in a most difficult position. These interests now did not have to lobby against our requests before the legislative committees; they controlled the requests at their source. At one legislative hearing upon our requests, one member of the committee actually asked me which side of the table a certain member of my Board was on. During one session of the Legislature when appropriation bills were being considered near the closing session late at night, the representatives of these financial interests pushed through a rider on the appropriations bill providing that no professional educator could serve as a member of the State Board of Education—the board that has general supervision over all the public schools of Texas, and recommends all the textbooks for the children in the public schools.

It was this tight politico-economic control of all education in Texas, and of The University of Texas in particular, that brought about my conflict with the Board of Regents to preserve the autonomy and educational integrity of the university. More details of this conflict are discussed in the chapters that follow.

THE

ISSUES

IN

THE

CONTROVERSY

AS

I

SAW

THEM

Although I was elected President of the University of Texas in late December 1938, I did not begin my official duties until June 1, 1939. The reason for the delay in assuming my duties was that I needed additional time to round out my responsibilities with the American Youth Commission of the American Council on Education, which I had been directing since 1935. I was formally inaugurated in the early part of December, 1939.

The first two years of my administration (1939-1941) were very happy and constructive ones for me. I used the time primarily to become acquainted with all aspects of the university's work and its far-reaching programs, and to formulate my ideas and plans for the future development of the university.

As a significant part of the inaugural activities we planned a large conference composed of outstanding educational leaders from the entire country and also many business and industrial leaders of Texas and elsewhere. The main purpose of this conference was to consider the major functions of a great state university and the role of such a university in the life of the society of which it is a part. I built my formal inaugural address on the ideas and conclusions of this conference.

I should like to indicate here that the conclusions of the inaugural conferences and the principles outlined in my inaugural address were very favorably received at that time. I can recall no adverse criticisms of the program as it was presented at that time. At least, no open or public criticisms were made of it. I was naturally quite happy about the whole situation, and had all kinds of encouragement and inspiration for the outstanding opportunities that lay ahead. All factors seemed to have approval, and were off to an auspicious start.

Hence, these first two years were not only pleasant, but were very constructive in planning and launching the program of my administration.

However, before these two years were over storm clouds were developing on the horizon. After Governor O'Daniel's re-election in 1940 it became quite clear that he had been taken into the camp of the "big interests" in Texas. It was during the interim between re-election and his second inauguration that he met with the group in Houston, described by Robert T. Bobbitt and Major Parten, and planned the take-over of the boards of control of all the educational institutions of Texas. Major Parten himself was one of Governor O'Daniel's targets, and was displaced at the next appointment period in January, 1941. His removal was a tragedy for The University of Texas, and for me personally.

Governor O'Daniel, in January, 1941, appointed two new Regents who were ultra-conservative socially, politically and economically. One was Orville Bullington, a lawyer and railroad magnate from Wichita Falls who had been the leader of the republican party in Texas for a number of years. Mr. Bullington was so extreme in his views that he and his fellow delegates were thrown out of the Chicago Republican Convention of 1944. The second appointee was a multimillionaire oil magnate of Houston, Dan Harrison, who had no conception of what a first-class university should be, and who was a close personal friend of Orville Bullington and took many of his ideas from him.

The point that I wish to emphasize here is that the changes

on the Board of Regents in January, 1941, were what really set in motion the controversy between me and the Regents.

The controversy begans as a difference of opinion over what personnel policies should be followed with regard to the faculty. The issues can be clarified and described by reference to official documents. Fortunately, abundant documentary materials are available to give a clear picture of all that happened.

Although the controversy developed over a period of two or more years, it was not brought into the open until a statement prepared by myself was read to the faculty in a specially called session on October 12, 1944. The press was also invited to this meeting of the faculty, and the Regents were informed in advance of the contents or the statement; each Regent was sent a copy of the statement prior to its presentation. It was mailed to each of them in time for each to receive it by the time the statement was to be delivered.

This statement was made to the faculty and to the public because I was convinced after long efforts with the Regents that no other action was left to me.

THE UNIVERSITY OF TEXAS
Office of the President
Austin

October 12, 1944

TO THE FACULTY OF THE UNIVERSITY OF TEXAS:

I have asked you to meet in special session today in order that I might make a personal report to you on the controversy between the Board of Regents and the University Administration. I am making this report to you because I am aware of your vital interest in and concern with the affairs of The University of Texas. You have expressed this concern to me in many ways, through letters, telephone calls and personal conversations. I am at the same time releasing this report to the press for the information of the entire citizenship of Texas who also have a fundamental and vital interest in the issues involved. Many of them, too, have expressed their concern to me by letters, telegrams and telephone calls from every section of the state. Interest and concern have also been shown to a marked degree by the students of the university who themselves have much at stake in the outcome of any fundamental issue that affects vitally the life and welfare of their university.

A critical situation has developed between the University Administration and the Board of Regents. I am sure you will appreciate my reluctance to take the step which I am now taking. For one in my position the last thing that one would want to do would be to effect a breach between himself and his governing board. I assure you and them that over a period of five years I have done all that I could possibly do to work in harmony and in cooperation with the Board of Regents and to prevent any issues arising between us that would affect adversely the welfare of The University of Texas. Matters have developed to the point, however, where I believe that only a statement from me will bring the facts and issues underlying the current situation into the open. I believe that you, the students, and the people of Texas have every right to these facts and that the publication of them now is the only way through which these issues can perhaps be resolved. These are issues which belong to the entire citizenship of Texas. The matter is of such great consequence to the welfare of the university that I am impelled to make this report. I regard it as my duty and obligation.

For a long time there has existed disharmony between the Regents and the Administration, and the events of the last few days have only served to bring the issues to a head. The recent effort on the part of one or more members of the Board of Regents to set limitations upon my activities and the attempt to restrict the freedom of the President of the university, either directly or indirectly, is only the last in a long series of restrictive actions that have been attempted by, or actually incorporated into, the policy of the present Board of Regents and that have violated long established principles of university administration.

The whole matter boils down to two major issues. These issues are clear-cut and fundamental. They are:

(1) The issue of the freedom of the university without which it is not a university and can never become a university of the first class. This is basic to everything else.

(2) The issue of the recognition of the proper relationships between a governing board and the executive and administrative officers of the university. No large organization of this kind can function effectively unless all parties concerned understand and observe the proper interrelationships between the functions that are appropriate to each level of administration.

Fundamental in the issue of "freedom" is the question of the attitude that the university authorities, whether administrators or Regents, should have in carrying out their responsibilities of supervision and administration. For centuries, universities worthy of the name have been the meeting place for conflicting ideas. It is well that this is true, for conflicts in ideas, when resolved through the orderly processes of society, lead to human progress. An idea, if contrary to prevailing opinions, usually gains more momentum when forced into subterranean channels through repression. I believe that history proves that the strength of democracy lies in tolerance, whether in the market place, or in public offices, or in institutions of higher learning. As the late Justice Oliver Wendell Holmes stated in a classic dissenting opinion:

> "Persecution for the expression of opinions seems to me perfectly logical. If you have no doubt of your premises or your power and want a certain result with all your heart you naturally express your wishes in law and sweep away all opposition. To allow opposition by speech seems to indicate that you think the speech impotent, as when a man says that he has squared the circle, or that you do not care wholeheartedly for the result, or that you doubt either your power or your premises. But when men have realized that time has upset many fighting faiths, they may come to believe even more than they believe the very

foundations of their own conduct that the ultimate good desired is better reached by free trade in ideas—that the best test of truth is the power of the thought to get itself accepted in the competition of the market, and that truth is the only ground upon which their wishes safely can be carried out. That at any rate is the theory of our Constitution."

There are, of course, individual actions and activities occurring in universities that a particular individual may not like. It is most important, however, that a tolerant attitude be taken toward these actions and activities which are not actually dangerous or subversive, in order that the basic principles for which universities stand shall not be destroyed for the sake of satisfying a passing whim or in compliance with the dictates of a temporary majority.

I shall attempt now to present to you in as definite, as objective and concise a manner as I am able, a list or catalogue of a number of restrictive measures, actual or attempted, as well as expressed attitudes, which the Board, or individual members of the Board, have taken during my administration and which to my mind violate the principles inherent in the two major issues previously stated. In giving examples to illustrate these violations, I have mentioned specific incidents and individuals by name in order to make the record clear. In referring to individual members of the Board, I have done so in their official capacities only and the statements concerning them are not intended to be in any way or to the slightest extent a personal attack upon any of them.

1.

Shortly after I became President of the university on June 1, 1939, Mr. Weinert of Seguin called upon me in person and requested me not to renominate Professor J. C. Dolley for the chairmanship of the Athletic Council. This request on his part naturally came as a great surprise to me. I had thought that the athletic troubles which the university had had for a number of years had been successfully solved and that Mr. Dolley's leadership as chairman of the faculty committee was largely responsible for the solution of this long-continuing athletic problem. Furthermore, this is a good example of a member of the Board stepping over into the field of administration which is clearly the prerogative of the executive officer of the university. If a president cannot have the privilege of appointing the members of the faculty committees without interference from his governing board, there is not much that he can do in a constructive way. The Board, of course, has a right to expect that a president will use his appointive power in harmony with sound judgment and the good of the university—that he will appoint persons in whom there can be no question about their moral character, their efficiency in their work or their loyalty to the ideals of the institution and the society of which it is a part. Mr. Weinert raised none of these points against Professor Dolley. The only basis of his request as I understood it was that Dr. Dolley was personally unsatisfactory to him. After long consideration and much worry over the matter I felt compelled to say to Mr. Weinert that I could not in good faith replace Mr. Dolley as chairman of this committee. I had to say that to the Board and request his reappointment.

2.

Another good example of a board member's failure to understand and recognize the proper province of executive leadership is a statement from

Regent Strickland in a letter addressed to me under date of March 16, 1943, in reply to a request which I had made of him to withdraw a resolution which he had presented to the Board changing the tenure rule. He says:

> "I doubt the wisdom and propriety of you, as President of the University, urging or suggesting that a member of the Board of Regents refrain from doing anything whatsoever that such Regent might think proper in connection with the performance of his official duties. The effect of your letter is to suggest and practically urge that I withdraw this statement before it is acted upon by the Board."

3.

A former member of the Board of Regents, at his first budget meeting at which the budget for the year 1940-41 was being considered, made a motion to strike from the budget the salary of Dr. R. H. Montgomery, Professor of Economics, and thus in effect eliminate him by a procedure which was in complete violation of the Board's rules of academic tenure. Fortunately, he was not able to secure enough support in the Board to accomplish this purpose, but the complete disregard which he exhibited for our long-standing principles of academic tenure was a source of great concern to me. At this meeting of the Board he exhibited and read to the Board excerpts from stenographic notes of Dr. Montgomery's addresses.

4.

At the same meeting of the Board of Regents, Mr. Lutcher Stark presented a motion to eliminate Dean Shelby, Mr. Roy Bedichek and Mr. R. J. Kidd from the Division of Extension of the university. Mr. Stark's reason for urging their removal was due, as he said, to the part which they had played in changing the rules of the Interscholastic League which affected the eligibility of his two sons who were then seniors in Orange High School. I pled with Mr. Stark not to take this action and told him that we had ample rules covering cases of this sort, and that if he would present this charge against these men in the regular manner I would invoke the rules of the Board of Regents and arrange for these men to have a hearing on these charges. Mr. Stark refused to do this. This matter was carried over until a later meeting of the Board. In the meantime Mr. Stark contacted me and demanded that I support him in his efforts to remove these men from the university without recourse to a hearing. I told him that I could not and would not take such action and urged him that if he had a grievance against these men to present it in the regular way. Upon my refusal to comply with his demand, he said to me, "Well, if you do not do this, I am through." I replied, "What do you mean by your statement 'I am through'?" His reply to me was. "I am going to fight you like hell." At the meeting of the Board of Regents which followed I had, of course, to recommend these men's re-employment. Mr. Stark made a motion for their dismissal but it did not receive the support of the Board.

5.

In the summer of 1942 the Board of Regents refused to re-employ three economic instructors: J. Fagg Foster, Wendell C. Gordon and W. N. Peach. Facts relating to this episode have already been widely published, and space will not permit a recital of the details of this affair.

It is significant, however, that the action taken by the Regents has resulted in an investigation by the American Association of University Professors who have raised with the Regents the question of their violation of the principles of academic freedom. This matter is still pending between the Regents and the American Association of Univeristy Professors and is scheduled for discussion between them at the next meeting of the Board at the end of this month.

6.

Another issue involving the principle of freedom of thought and teaching was the action by the Board of Regents at their meeting on January 8, 1943, removing the novel, *U.S.A.*, by John Dos Passos, from the supplementary reading list in a course in sophomore English. Prior to the consideration of this matter by the Regents, the administration, in conference with the Chairman of the English Department and the departmental committee in charge of this course, had secured the voluntary cooperation of the department in omitting this book from the reading list at the beginning of the next semester. This was done because certain people, including Regents, had expressed objections to the nature of the material in the book. The English Committee very promptly said that if there were any serious objection to the book they would be glad to omit it from the reading list. The Board, however, took up the matter subsequently, conducted a hearing at which the Chairman of the English Department and the committee responsible for this course were present, and for two hours or more the members of the Board of Regents, led by the Chairman, Judge Bickett, attempted to place the responsibility for the placing of this book on the reading list upon some one individual. During this investigation the statement was made numerous times by certain Board members that if responsibility could be placed upon any single individual for this book's being on the reading list, the Regents would remove this individual from the faculty of the university. The members of the committee stoutly maintained that no single individual was responsible and that it was placed on the reading list as a result of committee action. The only action, therefore, which was left to the Board was the passage of a resolution prohibiting the use of this book on any reading list in any course given in the University. It is worthy of note that this book has been selected within recent weeks as one of the five greatest literary productions of this generation in American literature.

7.

Over a considerable period of time during the late summer and fall of 1942, Regent Strickland conferred with me personally and by letter insisting that there were a great many unpatriotic attitudes held and activities undertaken by the members of the faculty of The University of Texas and that the faculty members holding these attitudes and engaging in these activities should be discovered and removed from the university. I assured him on numerous occasions that that was not the case, that we were keeping in close touch with these matters through the duly constituted governmental agencies set up to deal with such matters and that we were confident that the faculty of the university was loyal and patriotic. In spite of this assurance he insisted upon subjecting all of us to a patriotism test in the form of a questionnaire prepared by himself and to be submitted to every faculty member and employee of the university. I did all that I could to prevail upon him not to take this step. I argued further with him that all of us in the employ of the university were required to take a "loyalty" oath that was as strong as the oath which he had taken as a Regent and that I believed all of us had subscribed to that oath in good faith. In spite of my protesting with him about the matter, he did, on his own initiative, present such a resolution to the Board at its meeting in January 1943, and exhibited the questionnaire that he wished to require all members of the faculty and the staff to fill out. I felt compelled to ask the Board not to adopt such a procedure and fortunately it was not done.

8.

As soon as the Board refused to adopt Mr. Strickland's patriotism test, he removed from his pocket and presented to the Board the following resolution which in effect would have destroyed completely the principle of academic tenure,* a long-established and recognized policy in all first-class educational institutions:

BE IT RESOLVED by the Board of Regents of The University of Texas that the *Rules and Regulations of the Board of Regents for the Government of The University of Texas*, Sixth Edition, adopted by the Board of Regents on March 14, 1936, be amended in the following manner, to wit: That Section 3, of Chapter I, Part II, page 16, of the *Rules and Regulations of the Board of Regents for the Government of the University of Texas*, Sixth Edition, be amended by striking out the following paragraph:

"A professor or associate professor may be summarily suspended for grave cause pending investigation but will not be dismissed against his will except for cause stated in writing and until a special advisory committee of five mature and judicially-minded members of the General Faculty, appointed by the President for the purpose, shall have heard him fully, investigated all of the relevant facts, arrived at findings and recommendations, and submitted a full written statement of the Complaint and Grievance Committee of the Board of Regents. This Committee, together with the whole Board, will give serious consideration to the findings and recommendations of the Faculty Committee before any possible exercise of the power of dismissal."

It should be noted that this resolution did not attempt to modify the rule of the Regents affecting the right of professors and associate professors to have charges preferred against them and the right to be heard on these charges by a committee of their peers, but the resolution would have abolished completely this right. I make this point here because it was later contended by some of the Regents that they did not intend to abolish this right completely but only wanted to revise it in such a way as to bring it into harmony with the law and the legal responsibilities of the Board of Regents.

---

*By tenure in the university is meant, in essence, that when a member of the faculty has reached the grade of associate professor or full professor, it is assumed that he will be re-appointed in his position year after year so long as he does his work well and does not violate the principles of personal integrity or engage in disloyal or subversive activities, and that he will not be discharged from the university against his will without having the right of written charges preferred against him and an opportunity to have a full and complete hearing upon these charges.

Nothing that the Regents had done up to this point so alarmed me as this attempt to abolish our rule of faculty tenure. I was so disturbed about it that I felt that every possible effort had to be made to prevent the adoption of this resolution. I therefore requested the Board to permit time enough for the consideration of this important matter and to give me and the faculty opportunity to present the case for faculty tenure to the Board. This privilege was granted and I appointed a committee of the faculty to study and discuss this matter with the Board. The committee, after meeting with me, instructed me to present the case for this principle to the Regents in as strong terms as I could. I did this in a four-page letter addressed to the Regents under date of February 10, 1943. This led to further discussion of the problem, but I think you would be interested to know that during this discussion Regent Strickland characterized our system of faculty participation through budget councils in the governing of The University of Texas as "a self-perpetuating feudal system." Also on numerous occasions, too numerous to mention, certain members of the Board thrust jeers and jibes at our system of tenure and referred to it and the American Association of University Professors, who protect the principle, in such terms as "the professors' C.I.O. Labor Union." In all discussions of this matter I have felt that the Regents had no respect at all for the principle. They continued to urge the adoption of Mr. Strickland's resolution, and went so far as to refer it to the Attorney General, claiming that the system was illegal. We had, therefore, to fight for the principle through the Attorney General's department. Again I had to request permission of the Board for me and the faculty committee to present a brief to the Attorney General expressing our point of view in defense of the tenure system. We were permitted to do this, and a faculty committee composed of Dr. John W. Calhoun, Dr. E. C. Barker, and Judge Robert W. Stayton and I prepared such a brief and presented it to the Attorney General. In this brief your committee made four contentions to the Attorney General in support of the principle. I am happy to report to you that the Attorney General sustained your committee's contentions on every single point and thus established the principle firmly in Texas law.

Following this favorable opinion of the Attorney General, members of the Regents still insisted that the rule had to be revised. I requested this same committee to work with the Regents in an attempt to make a satisfactory revision of the rule. This revision was finally adopted by the Board. In its present form it leaves considerable doubt as to whether or not it is an adequate protection of faculty rights. The local chapter of the Association of University Professors submitted the revised rule to the Council of the American Association of University Professors asking whether or not the rule in its present form met the standards of the Association. The Association replied under date of November 18, 1943, as follows:

"Tenure revision weakens tenure provisions of university and does not conform to 1940 statement of principles."

The effort on the part of the Regents to abolish this principle of faculty tenure has had, and will continue to have, several serious adverse effects upon the university. In the first place, it raises in the minds of all of us a serious question as to the present rights and status of members of the faculty in the university. In the second place, it has made and will continue to make the recruiting of new members of the faculty difficult. Men of intellectual ability will hesitate to accept a position on the faculty of the university unless our practices in all respects conform to the best traditions of academic freedom and tenure. In the third place, the effect of this attitude of the Board upon the attitudes of our faculty will inevitably be that many faculty members, when receiving offers to go to other places, will be far more inclined to accept those offers than they would have been had they felt adequately protected here.

9.

Another serious breach was opened between the administration and the Regents with the removal of Mr. Arthur L. Brandon from his position as Director of Public Relations for the university. Before I was elected to the presidency of the university the matter of the university's public relations had been given long and serious study by both the faculty and the Board of Regents, and the conclusion had been mutually arrived at that one of the great needs of the university was a well-developed program of public relations under a capable director. When I was approached about the presidency of the university I was told these things and promised that I might have the privilege of establishing such a department and of selecting a capable and full-time director for it. To that position I brought Mr. Brandon, who had demonstrated through years of experience an outstanding ability in this field and who was then recognized as one of the few best men in this work among the colleges and universities in the United States. Mr. Brandon joined the staff in September 1939, and for four years did an excellent piece of work in helping all of us interpret the university to the people of Texas and in improving the press relations of the university and its prestige among the people generally, both in Texas and throughout the nation. I was, therefore, astounded when the Board removed him from this position without bringing a single charge against him and denied his own request for an opportunity to come before the Board to be heard. The Board has a committee of public relations, the chairman of which is Regent Strickland. Never at any time did this committee call upon Mr. Brandon and investigate or consult with him concerning the work that he was doing, although on numerous occasions Mr. Brandon invited their interest and cooperation. It is inevitable that such treatment by the Regents of members of the staff of the university cannot help but have an unwholesome effect upon the attitude and morale of the entire group, whether employee or teacher.

There was another event connected with Mr. Brandon's dismissal that illustrates an unfortunate practice of the present Board of Regents. Without my knowing anything about it, a member of the Board of Regents, Mr. Bullington, called Mr. William McGill on the telephone the night before the precipitate dismissal of Mr. Brandon occurred and told Mr. McGill that the Board was going to change the Director of Public Relations at its meeting the next day and asked Mr. McGill if he would take the position. Mr. McGill, according to his personal statement to me about the matter, told Mr. Bullington that he could not take the position under these circumstances. Mr. Bullington replied, in effect, "Well, you would take it, would you not, if the Board were to draft you for the place?" Mr. McGill's reply was, "No, I could not take it under any circumstances." In spite of Mr. McGill's statement, at the meeting of the Board the following morning when Mr. Brandon was dismissed, the same resolution which dismissed him called for the appointment of Mr. McGill to that place. I, of course, had again to protest this action as a gross violation of the rights of a member of the staff on the one hand, and also as a gross interference with the rights of the President to nominate members of the staff. The Board in this way acted directly and independently of the President in such a way as almost completely to undermine the relations that ought normally to exist between the Regents and the administration.

It should be noted also with regard to the matter of public relations that the Attorney General's department had, previous to this action of the Board, rendered a favorable opinion stating that the university was well within its rights under the law to establish such a division in the university and to use public funds for that purpose. In spite of this, Judge Bickett argued that he opposed the university's having a Department of Public Relations at all on the theory that the university had no right to use public funds for such purpose.

10.

In another important respect the Regents have shown their disposition to restrict freedom of research and thought at the university. This is in the area of social science research. They have been very careful to scrutinize every project that was presented in the social sciences by members of the faculty to make sure that it was the type of research they could approve. Whereas they have approved all, or practically all, projects for research presented in the field of the natural sciences, they have turned down many requests for research funds, even though these funds were available from legislative grant for research purposes, for members of the faculty in the social sciences. For example, at one meeting of the Board on June 27, 1942, the following projects which had been duly recommended by the Research Council of the University and the Dean of the Graduate School were disapproved by the Board of Regents:

(1) Project #3: Request for the appropriation of $44.12 to C. M. Rosenquist for aid in publication by *Southwestern Social Science Quarterly* of articles by members of University faculty, from the 1941-42 budget of the University Research Institute. Motion for disapproval by Bickett, seconded by Strickland.

(2) Project #3: Request for $120 for same project and purpose as described in (1) above, from 1942-43 budget of the University Research Institute. Motion for disapproval by Bickett, seconded by Strickland.

(3) Project #65: Request for the appropriation of $600 to C. T. McCormich for continued publication of additional issues of *Texas Law Review* so as to increase opportunities for research publications by the members of the law faculty in the *Law Review*, from the 1942-1943 budget of the University Research Institute. Motion for disapproval by Bickett, seconded by Bullington.

(4) Project #40: Request for the appropriation of $450 for research assistance to G. W. Stumberg for the continuation of study of phases of criminal law or criminal procedure which may be in need of reform. Motion for disapproval by Bickett, seconded by Strickland.

(5) Project #72: Request for the appropriation of $600 to R. W. Stayton for the continuation of Texas market study for legal services, from the 1942-43 budget of the University Research Institute. Motion for disapproval by Bickett, seconded by Strickland.

(6) Project #79: Request for the appropriation of $2,212 for assistance and supplies to Harry E. Moore for the continuation of the study of war booms in three Texas towns, from the 1942-1943 budget of the University Research Institute. Motion for disapproval by Strickland, seconded by Bickett.

(7) Project #92: Request for the appropriation of $450 for research and assistance to D. L. Clark for work on a biography of Charles Brockden Brown, from the 1942-1943 budget of the University Research Institute. Motion for disapproval by Bickett, seconded by Strickland.

(8) Project #93: Request for the appropriation of $450 for research assistance to J. H. Frederick for a study of the development and present status of air transportation in Latin America, from the 1942-1943 budget of the University Research Institute. Motion for disapproval by Bickett, seconded by Bullington.

It was at the last meeting of the Board on September 29, 1944, that the Regents refused a research project for Professor G. L. Joughlin in which he asked for $150 for funds to carry on a study on the effects of the Sacco-Vanzetti case upon American literature. The Board refused this request with some such statement as, "Justice Frankfurter has already made martyrs of these two men and there is no reason to study the matter any further." It should be noted that this refusal to grant these funds was not due to a lack of funds, but to the fact that this type of research was not thought desirable by the Regents. This is certainly placing limitations and restrictions upon the freedom of members of the faculty to follow their intellectual interests.

11.

For a long time there has been a great need for a School of Social Work in the university to train people for many types of jobs now available in the state of Texas that require professional training in social casework methods. The university has been petitioned time and time again by interested groups to develop a graduate school for this training in the southwest area. There is no opportunity in this entire southwest region for people to secure this training. The Regents have constantly refused to approve the beginning of this school or to allow us to request the Legislature for funds to support it. The only reason apparently for their disapproval is the fear that such a school would train bureaucrats and socialists.

12.

A similar type of thinking has been applied to the Bureau of Municipal Research. The Bureau carries on researches and investigations into the problems of municipalities. It also has in the past conducted institutes for the training of tax assessors-collectors. In 1942 this Bureau published a study entitled *Municipal Electric Utilities in Texas.* In this study considerable attention was devoted to some of the advantages of municipally owned utilities. There was considerable objection to this study on the part of certain members of the Board and there was a serious threat to eliminate funds from the budget for the support of this Bureau. It took a great deal of persuasion to prevent them from eliminating the Bureau altogether.

13.

One of the most important aids that a university can give to the professional growth of its faculty is that of permitting them to attend their national professional organization meetings. The University of Texas is quite far removed from the other intellectual centers of the United States and it is important for our faculty to have the opportunity to attend their professional meetings in order to keep up their professional interest and contacts and the stimulation that results from such contacts. It had been the policy of this administration to encourage as much as possible the attendance of the faculty at these meetings. The Legislature had recognized this need by permitting us to use university funds to pay traveling expenses. The Board of Regents at its meeting on September 25, 1942, passed a resolution making it the general policy of the institution not to allow the use of university funds for this purpose. It is, of course, possible to have abuses under the former policy and to spend funds in a way that is not justified, but on the other hand it seems an equally unwise policy to eliminate the practice altogether.

14.

One of the most serious differences that has arisen between the Administration and the Board has been over the matter of appropriations from the Legislature. The university has never had adequate funds to support a first-class university. It has been particularly limited in funds for faculty salaries. During the meeting of the last Legislature members of the Board of Regents made repeated attempts to get us to reduce our appropriation requests to that of a "minimum budget" instead of trying to help us get funds for an adequate budget. Members of the Board themselves urged that we reduce our appropriation requests as much as twenty-two percent below what we had already requested of the Legislature. We had requested some $230,000 less than we had received the previous biennium. To have reduced it twenty-two percent as urged by some of the Regents would have been a serious financial handicap for the university. This attitude on the part of the Regents proved a serious handicap to us in the securing of funds from the Legislature. An incident which occurred in our hearing before the Senate Committee will illustrate this difficulty. In this hearing a Regent, Mr. Strickland, who is the chairman of the Legislative Committee of the Board of Regents, was present and made a talk to the Senate Committee. After he had finished his talk one of the senators addressed me and said to this effect, "Mr. President, I should like to ask you a question." "Certainly, Senator," I replied, "what is it?" He said, "I should like to ask you which side of the table Judge Strickland is on."

15.

Another serious difference arose between the administration and the Regents over the policy followed by the Regents for a number of months of holding executive sessions of the Board from which the Administration was excluded. Such a practice cannot help but be interpreted as a lack of confidence on the part of the Board in the Administration. Since the Board of Regents is a public body it is fair to assume that when they meet they are meeting for the purpose of considering the welfare of the university. Since no one is more responsible for the welfare of the institution than its President, it is a serious breach of courtesy and sound policy for the governing board to exclude the President from its executive sessions. That policy has been recently modified but it did much to create a lack of confidence between the Board and the Administration.

16.

Since the President of the university has no legal status and no legal authority, he is dependent for his effectiveness upon the observance by the governing board of sound principles of administration. If these sound principles covering the relationship between the Regents and the President become a mere figurehead and his authority and prestige are virtually destroyed. It is at this point that another serious breach has existed between the Regents and the Administration. The Medical School controversy, if written up in all of its details, would provide a classic example in American higher education of how Regents ought not to act. A large part of the unpleasantness that has existed in the Medical School situation has arisen from the fact that sound administrative policies were not followed. A few examples will illustrate this point.

To begin with, Dean Spies was not selected by a former Board in a proper manner. The Board of Regents had a committee appointed to work with a faculty and alumni committee for the selection of a dean. This worked very well up to the point of bringing Dean Spies to Galveston for an interview. While he was there the Chairman of the Regent's Medical Committee gave a luncheon honoring Dr. Spies for the Medical Committee of the Regents and the faculty and ex-students of the Medical Branch in Galveston. At this luncheon, greatly to the amazement and surprise of all those present, it was announced by the Chairman of the Medical Committee that Dr. Spies had been selected as the new Dean of the Medical School, although the matter had not been acted upon by the Committees involved or by the Board of Regents.

After a year and a half of serious, conscientious effort on the part of the President and the Board to deal with a highly unsatisfactory situation in Galveston, some new Regents were appointed in January 1941. Among these Regents were Mr. Orville Bullington of Wichita Falls and Mr. Dan Harrison of Houston. Sometime shortly after their selection, without ever mentioning it to the President or discussing it with the Dean of the Medical Branch, these two Regents went to Galveston and made a personal "survey" of the medical situation. They spent a day and a half or two days in Galveston interviewing various members of the faculty and citizens of Galveston. In this "survey" they seemed certain that they had found the answer to our problems in Galveston and a short time later, joining with certain other members of the Board, sent an ultimatum to me as President that I should not renominate Dean Spies at the forthcoming meeting of the Board of Regents on July 9, 1941, and that if I did renominate him they would have to vote him down.

It should be noted that this demand on the part of the Regents came after great progress had been made in straightening out the affairs of the Medical School in Galveston. A very complex administrative tangle had been cleared up. The John Sealy Hospital, which had been leased for many years to the City of Galveston, had been returned to the university for management so that it could be coordinated with the Medical School and thus become a far more effective teaching hospital. After a year's study by faculty committees, aided by committees of doctors representing county and state medical societies from various parts of the state, a thoroughly modern program of medical education was proposed for the Medical School in Galveston. This program received almost universal approval by the medical profession in Texas and our request for adequate funds to finance it was supported strongly by them in the Legislature. Whereas the Legislature had been appropriating only slightly in excess of $300,000 a year for all purposes for the Medical Branch in Galveston, the Legislature in 1941, prior to the ultimatum spoken of above, appropriated approximately $1,000,000 a year for the operation of the Medical Branch and the John Sealy Hospital, of which $250,000 was for the Hospital. This was the first time that state funds had been secured for the operation of the Hospital. Thus the ultimatum of the Board members not to reappoint Dean Spies came at the time of the greatest success for the Medical Program that had been achieved by any administration in the history of the university. I did everything possible to persuade the Board not to take this action. As a matter of fact, I pled with them for more than a week not to do it. However, my recommendations and my pleadings were rejected and on July 8, 1941, the Board announced to the public its intention not to reemploy Dean Spies, but said that the matter would be finally determined at a later meeting on July 26. In the interval between these two meetings a veritable avalanche of protests from the medical profession in Texas descended upon the Regents. The sentiment among the medical profession for Dean Spies was very strong at that time and the pressure upon the Board increased to such an extent that when the Board met again on July 26 it reversed its former decision and re-employed Dean Spies. Thus, I had seen a Board reject my recommendations and within less than three weeks' time, under nothing but sheer group pressure, reverse themselves. Since Dean Spies was reappointed under pressure and against the real desire of the Board, the Regents did not support either him or me in the months that followed, and their refusal to do so led to one crisis after another until a year later the situation had become so intolerable that there was nothing that could be done except to get a new administration for the Medical School.

Since I have received a great deal of criticism for my support of Dean Spies, I should like to make my position in this matter perfectly clear. In the first place, I did not hire Dean Spies, as many people seem to believe; but since he was the Dean of one of the important divisions of the university I felt it my duty and in line with my usual policy to support him insofar as I was able and to try to give his administration a chance to succeed.

When a new dean was to be selected the Board made another serious error. Instead of following the normal procedure of allowing the President of the university to nominate a dean to the Regents, the Board set the President aside and called upon a committee of doctors in the state to advise the Board on the selection of a new dean. This is a most unsound policy of university administration, since outside committees of this character are not composed of responsible administrative officers of the institution. Yet this was the procedure followed by the Regents in this case. Furthermore, after a new dean and vice-president was selected, the Board continued, in effect, to disregard the President with respect to Medical School matters. The President's recommendations concerning

Medical School matters were overruled so often that he was forced in effect to accept every recommendation submitted by the officials of the Medical School.

For more than a year I had tried to persuade the Board of Regents to make a thorough-going and objective survey of the medical situation in Texas and to plan a long-range program for the development of medical education in this state. A similar recommendation was made to the Board of Regents by the members of the University Development Board in October 1943. The Board of Regents, after much effort on Regent Strickland's part to prevent the question of location to be included in the survey, finally passed a resolution authorizing a survey to be made in which the question of location might be considered. At this point another administrative mistake was made. Such a survey normally should be directed by the President of the university as the Executive Officer of the Board. This, however, was not done. Instead the Medical Committee of the Board of Regents was charged with responsibility for making the survey and requested to call upon the President, the Vice-President of the Medical Branch and others for any help that they might need. Months passed and nothing was done toward making this survey, although I continued to urge it upon the Regents. Finally, on June 30, 1944, the Chairman of the Medical Committee, Mr. Weinert, wrote me and requested me to make a report to the Committee upon the entire medical situation and to present whatever recommendations I desired to make. In compliance with this request, I presented such a report to the Regents at their meeting on July 15. This report made some far-reaching recommendations, including the removal of the Medical School from Galveston to Austin. That part of my report was referred by the Board to the Medical Committee for further study and investigation. On September 29, the Medical Committee made a report to the Board of Regents in which it purported to have made a study of my recommendations and to have canvassed the situation thoroughly from every point of view. In this report of the Medical Committee every recommendation that I had made was turned down with no mention of the arguments which I had advanced to support my recommendations. Furthermore, the Committee did not allow me to meet with them to discuss their report, and when their report was presented to the Board my attempted discussion of it was rather rudely interrupted by one member.

The further facts emphasize how inadequately the Medical Committee carried out its task. In the first place, it recommended the return of the College of Pharmacy to Galveston and the members of the Committee admitted when asked that they had not discussed this matter with a single pharmacist in Texas or with a single member of the faculty of the College of Pharmacy or with the Dean of the College. In the second place, the amazing statement was made by one member of the committee in presenting the report to the effect that, "We have not found a single doctor in Texas who is in favor of moving the Medical School from Galveston to Austin." I offered the Board my personal files which contain many letters from prominent doctors favoring my proposal.

Such conduct on the part of a responsible Board of a great university is inexcusable. They have failed to meet their responsibilities to all the future medical students who will attend the school and to the people of Texas as well. It is my opinion that they have acted upon motives other than objective study of the needs of Texans. This is not the type of leadership which Texas wants and deserves. This type of conduct will wreck any administration in the world.

If I were to attempt to summarize the entire controversy, I would say that my five years of experience with these matters convinces me that the heart of the trouble arises out of the fact that the university is controlled by a group of persons who represent almost entirely one attitude of mind and one group of interests in the state; and that they have tried in numerous ways to impose their point of view upon the university and to restrict the freedom of those who have other points of view; and because I have felt that not only their point of view but all points of view should be protected in the university I have had to oppose many of their actions in the interests of maintaining the integrity of thought and expression in the university. Since in so acting I have often been placed in the position of opposing them they have turned their opposition upon me and have resorted to numerous violations of the principles of good administration as a means of achieving their ends. We are, thus, confronted with the central issue which every state university encounters. It is the question of whether or not our state universities can be operated in ways that will guarantee their essential freedom from undue political interference, without which they can never achieve the status of great universities.

This recital of a long list of differences between the University Administration and the Regents might lead to the belief that the breach is so wide and so deep that it cannot be healed. I do not feel this to be the case. The members of the Board of Regents are all very influential citizens of Texas, and there is much that they can do for the university. It would be my greatest joy to work cooperatively with them in behalf of The University of Texas. I am glad to offer publicly to the Regents my willingness to cooperate with them in working out these differences. I am confident that we can work successfully together if they will do two things: first, that they recognize, guarantee and protect the essential freedoms in the university; that is freedom of thought, freedom of research and investigation, and freedom of expression. Without these freedoms the institution will not be and cannot become a real or great university. Second, that they recognize and observe those legitimate functions of administrative authorities, which, by all human experience and tradition, have been assigned to responsible executives in every type of human organization. I am sure that all of the Regents, experienced as they are in the management of large affairs, would not tolerate for one moment in their own businesses some of the methods which they have followed in the administration of the university. On my part, I am perfectly willing and happy to recognize the legitimate and legal authority of the Board with respect to its broad policy determining functions.

The President, under present regental rules, is supposed to be the professional advisor to the Board. It is the President's function to study the needs of the institution and to recommend actions for the Board's consideration. It is well known that a lay Board cannot effectively perform these functions. A Board cannot run the university. It must do this through trained and competent executive leadership. It must trust and support that leadership. It is the Board's duty and function to examine carefully the plans and recommendations made by its professional officers and after having done so to accept, modify or reject them as their wisdom and responsibility dictate. Once a policy has been determined in this way it is the President's duty and responsibility to carry it out to the best of his ability and the Board should rightly hold him accountable for its proper execution. The Board should never attempt to formulate a policy, however, without seeking the advice of the President, for once a policy has been determined, the President then becomes responsible for its execution. The best and most effective results are obtained when policies are formulated cooperatively and jointly by the President and the Board to the end that every policy becomes in actuality a joint policy. Furthermore, a lay Board should not concern itself with the details of administration, for these require continuous attention. Only by adhering to these basic principles can any board and administration work together successfully.

I returned to Texas more than five years ago believing that the university offered the greatest opportunity for constructive service of any institution in the United States. I feel that that opportunity still exists.

REACTIONS TO MY CHARGES

The effects of my statement of October 12th were electric. The response of the faculty was appreciative and genuinely sincere and sympathetic, and brought profound satisfaction to me. One of the members of the faculty said of the meeting that it was the finest religious experience that he had ever had.

However, it was not that kind of an experience for the Regents. They were stunned and confused and angry. Their attitudes were described to me two days later by one of the editors of the *Dallas Morning News* in a long-distance telephone conversation, during which he said that my statement had "rocked them back on their heels."

There was, of course, much excitement and discussion everywhere about the situation, but the Regents made no attempt to reply to these charges. I had deliberately and definitely left the way open for some kind of negotiation with the Board. It was my hope that through the efforts of the faculty, the Ex-Students' Association and the public a solution could be worked out.

The Vice-President, Dr. Burdine, and I had prepared carefully a letter to the Regents and made proposals for a meeting. Nothing came out of these proposals. The Board did not accept our request for a meeting.

There were, however, immediate reactions from the students, the faculty, and the alumni association. The press of Texas also reacted vigorously to the situation. In order that the positions and actions of each of these groups may be adequately presented, I have let each group speak for itself. Fortunately, abundant records of these actions exist. Immediately following my dismissal by the Board of Regents on November 1, 1944, the Senate of the Texas Legislature appointed a committee to make a thorough investigation of the situation. This committee held sessions for approximately one week, and took about two thousand pages of sworn testimony. All interested groups and numerous individuals were called before this committee for testimony. The records of these hearings provide invaluable authoritative materials for the analysis of the conflict. I have, therefore, made extensive use of these records. This has required considerable use of direct quotations and some necessary duplication, but I feel that these quotations throw much light upon the conflict and aid in the understanding of it. I feel also that it is far better to permit these groups and individuals to speak for themselves than to present a digest and paraphrase of their statements. I have, therefore, drawn quite freely from these official statements from the faculty, the students, the alumni association, and have included a separate chapter devoted to the reactions of the press, including both the Texas press and a number of papers across the nation. This conflict soon became a national interest, and many of the leading papers of the nation editorialized about it.

Reactions of the Faculty

The reactions of the faculty were immediate and strongly in support of my administration and my policies. They passed several strong solutions, and appointed a committee to work with me and the Board in efforts to resolve the difficulties between us. They also worked with the ex-students' committee appointed for the same purpose.

Dr. Fred Duncalf, a long-time Professor of History, was one of the members of this faculty committee. Certain portions of his testimony before the Senate Investigating Committee appear below, and summarize the general reaction of the faculty:

The faculty has, I think, very generally been in rather complete sympathy with Dr. Rainey's ideas of a university, particularly the future university, and very glad to work with him and notwithstanding the war conditions, we've made considerable progress in planning to a certain extent because we were encouraged and stimulated to do that by Dr. Rainey; for example, there's been a General Policy Committee which has been working and planning for post-war conditions for, oh, two years; some of the recommendations have been already approved by the faculty. And so I think it's very natural that the faculty and Dr. Rainey have seen eye to eye, have been able to work together, and I think that's very important in this situation. After all, we've been told there are 400 or 500 faculty people and under the nine Regents, well, I should say eight Regents, to deal with and, as I say, the faculty doesn't quite understand, knowing Dr. Rainey, knowing this man, knowing his ideas, the faculty just can't quite understand why the Regents say they couldn't work with him. Now, maybe I know a little more about it than I did before going through all these experiences, but, frankly, I'm still perplexed. . . .

I simply wanted to tell you what the faculty has done. Of course, the faculty has been very greatly disturbed, you can understand that, and when the crisis approached, the faculty was anxious to do what it could to try and help the situation out, offering its services. So, on October 17th, the faculty met. Now, about the independence of the faculty, this meeting was called according to faculty rules, on petition of 15 or more members with no knowledge from above. The secretary of the faculty, who is the elected officer of the faculty, called a meeting together and then was chosen as acting chairman; at that meeting the faculty passed unanimously a vote of confidence in Dr. Rainey, also selected a nominating committee to choose a committee of eleven, and the committee of eleven among other groups held another meeting on October 24th. Well, this statement was approved by the faculty and at the same time [the faculty] chose a committee of three to seek to ask the Board of Regents to permit them to meet with them, with or without a committee of ex-students and, as you know, the request was granted and the faculty committee was present at both those series of meetings which was one, an adjourned meeting at Houston, where this statement was presented. Now, this statement was satisfactory, a very good statement from the faculty point of view. It's a statement to the people of Texas, the Board of Regents, and the President of The University of Texas. . . .

It represents, I would say, the best thought of the faculty and this was to be presented to the Board as a basis, you might say a basis for a possible settlement, although these were fundamental principles which the faculty were not prepared to yield on; that is, this is what we think is necessary, about tenure, about different functions, the President of the Board and faculty. . . . November 3rd, another faculty meeting was held in which three other, four other resolutions were passed. The first of those resolutions was a request to the Governor and asking him in making the appointments to the Board, the Members of the Board of Regents, to consult with the faculty committee and the ex-students' committee, in suggesting that he try to nominate Regents of variety of interests and occupations, and so forth. The second resolution passed at that meeting was another vote of confidence in Dr. Rainey, hoping that he would be returned to the office of the President of The University of Texas; and the third resolution was a sort of vote of confidence in Dr. Painter who had been very hesitant about accepting the position of Acting President; we felt it was necessary that he do that.

Activities of the Students

The students of the university were aroused over the actions of the Regents in removing the President, and took a very active part in trying to have me reinstated Their president attended the Regent's meeting in Houston, and cooperated with ex-students and faculty representatives in their mutual efforts to affect a reconciliation between the Regents and myself.

After the Regents' action, one of the Regents met a student representative in the hall of the hotel, and in defense of their action remarked to the student that if the students knew what the Regents knew, they (the students) would be on the Regents' side of the controversy. This led the students to call a mass meeting for the following Saturday morning in the Gregory Gymnasium on the Campus. Each Regent was sent a telegram inviting him, or her, to attend this meeting and explain the Regents' point of view. The gymnasium was packed with students who waited two hours for the Regents to appear. Not a single Regent responded to this invitation, and pictures were taken of the stage showing nine empty seats.

On the day before (Friday), the students organized and carried out their mass parade through the main streets of Austin carrying the black-draped coffin marked "Academic Freedom." In addition, a large part of the student body refused to go to classes for several days in protest of the Regents' action.

The Regents called their first meeting in Houston following the release of my statement on October 28-29, 1944. The fact that the meeting was held in Houston rather than at the regular meeting place in Austin is not without significance in the strategy of the Regents.

Activities of Ex-Students' Association

Then followed the two days at Houston, October 31 and November 1. What happened in these two days is a truly remarkable story. A part of this story was well told by Mr. W. H. Francis, President of the Ex-Students' Council. He related the incidents as follows:

On Sunday morning about 7:30, Judge Bickett sent me a telegram at Dallas saying that the Regents had called an Executive Committee meeting, an Executive Regents' meeting, for Tuesday morning in Houston and asking for a committee of ex-students to come down there and meet with them in the Executive meeting, which had been proferred in Exhibit "B." Well, we didn't even have the committee appointed and I couldn't get at it until Monday and the telegram was on Sunday, and the councilmen are living all over the State.

I finally just took the matter in hand and named a committee to go which was later confirmed or approved by the Council, and I decided that this committee should be the officers of the Association and a couple of others which was fairly representative not only of the group but geographically. Bobbitt, the Vice-President, lived in San Antonio; John McCurdy, the Executive Secretary, here in Austin; and I as President, in Dallas. And I named Herman Pipkin, attorney at Amarillo, who more or less represented that northwest, west section; Judge J. C. Hutcheson, at Houston, who had been presenting this before and who, as I said, is a very able and capable advocate of fair deals and square deals and knows a whole lot about what a university ought to be. And then we asked Hines Baker to serve on it, he living in Houston and, as I said before, Houston being somewhat of a hot spot for this meeting and what was transpiring at that particular time.

At any rate, this committee went down there and approached the executive hearing or meeting which the Regents had on this basis, on the basis that had been presented in Exhibit "B" with our committee and the committee from the faculty which was there and both committees elected and designated Judge Hutcheson to be the spokesman and represent us and present all matters which occurred outside and inside of the executive meeting of the Board. Our whole and total purpose throughout the whole meeting that lasted better than two days and the most part of two nights was to try to get the Board of Regents to agree to harmonize everything, get together with Dr. Rainey, wipe the slate clean, start over and run a university of the first class, we believing they could do it if they wanted to and we believing that Dr. Rainey was willing to cooperate and work with them to do it and to accomplish it.

In trying to work it out we proposed that there be set up a faculty committee by the Board of Regents who would sit as liaison committee or advisory committee with the President and the Board of Regents to discuss and work out all matters that might arise in which they jointly participated or individually participated, so that maybe decisions in the future could be worked out satisfactorily and everything move on nicely. All of us urged the Regents not to resign and, of course, that they continue with Dr. Rainey to run the university rightly so that it would be a university of the first class and continue to be.

After this long and tedious and tiresome session, the Regents held an executive session of their own to which none of us were admitted and out of that, and to my surprise and it was quite a shock, they fired Dr. Rainey and three of them resigned. They resigned like firecrackers popping and you couldn't tell where the next one was coming from and there were three more of the Regents [who] made statements so that they were quoted in the press and it was stated that they intended to resign. The three who [announced that they would] resign were Bullington and Mr .Schreiner, and Strickland. So, from that meeting we came back here and called a meeting of the Council of the Ex-Students' Association here in Austin to consider what was the best thing that we could do under existing conditions and, of course, we found the University Faculty and student body and the city of Austin in a turmoil and, as I say, a crisis in existence and tension terrific. We met and we had nearly all of the councilmen present from all over the State, one coming as far as from El Paso, one from Amarillo, two from the border at Brownsville and Laredo and Corpus Christi; they were here from all over the State and those who weren't here, by telephone and telegram or otherwise, ratified what the Council did here that day as being its action and what it considered was the best thing to be done for the State and the University and the Ex-Students' Association.

That action is reflected in a document which I have here and we can call it Exhibit "C," which was adopted, as I say, by a unanimous vote of the Council present, all members voting for it and all who were not here authorizing their names to be put on the document as indicating that they favored this statement. There was one man present who voted in favor of the document but who refused to sign it and after the request was made for him to sign the document, he said he could but requested that he be counted present and not voting but afterward . . . Judge Hutcheson stated that that gentleman said this was a perfectly fair statement and a solid basis and foundation of the Ex-Students' Council and Association and the State and University, you might say, to stand on as things existed then and as they exist today. [At this point the statement by the Ex-Students' Association was read into the record.]

STATEMENT ADOPTED BY UNANIMOUS VOTE OF THOSE PRESENT AT A SPECIAL MEETING OF THE EXECUTIVE COUNCIL OF THE EX-STUDENTS' ASSOCIATION HELD IN AUSTIN ON SATURDAY, NOVEMBER 4, 1944; ALSO SUBSCRIBED TO BY SEVERAL COUNCILMEN NOT PRESENT WHO ASKED THAT THEIR NAMES BE ADDED TO THE LIST OF THOSE PRESENT

The President of the Ex-Students' Association of The University of Texas acting in the emergency appointed a committee consisting of the President, First Vice-President and Executive Secretary of the Association and other members geographically selected to represent the Council at the meeting of the Board of Regents held in Houston on October 31 through November 1, such committee being composed of the following: W. H. Francis, Robert Lee Bobbitt, John A. McCurdy, J. C. Hutcheson, Jr., Hines H. Baker, and H. C. Pipkin. The faculty also appointed a committee consisting of Dr. Frederic Duncalf, Dr. T. S. Painter and Judge Robert W. Stayton, to meet with the Regents and the committee from the Council. The Ex-Students' Committee conferred with the Regents and the President during the two-day session of the Regents at Houston and earnestly and diligently sought to compose the differences between the

Regents and the President. These efforts were unsuccessful. The Regents discharged the President. Three of the Regents resigned. Three other Regents are reported to have declared their intention to resign. Up to this time the resignations of the latter three Regents have not been received by the Governor.

The Ex-Students' Committee and the Faculty Committee met with the Governor at Austin on November 2, at which meeting were present the President of the Students' Association and the Chairman of the Judiciary Council. The Ex-Students' Committee and the Faculty Committee recommended to the Governor that he accept the resignations of the six Regents and not reappoint them. They also outlined to him their views as to the type of men who should be appointed Regents.

It appears that the solution of the differences between the Regents and the American Association of University Professors and the Southern Association of Colleges and Secondary Schools will be made easier by the appointment of a new Board of Regents. This controversy may make it difficult, if not impossible, for the University to secure and retain adequate and competent research and teaching faculty and competent administrative personnel. Under the existing conditions the faculty and the student body are in turmoil, confusion and demoralization. In view of the above and the unfortunate conditions which now exist, it is the considered judgment of the Council, acting without partianship and with the best interest of the University in mind, that:

1. The three Regents who resigned are to be commended for such action.

2. It is to the best interest of the University that the remaining Regents who have served prior to October 30 should follow the lead of the others and resign immediately.

3. The Governor should immediately accept such resignations and not reappoint any of such Regents.

4. It is highly important to have constituted a Board of Regents with all new members who will take over the government of the University and begin afresh, free from the controversies that have existed. To this end the Governor is urged to give the most careful consideration to the appointment of Regents who will be free from the controversy and from biases or prejudices produced by it, and who will be persons who possess the other qualifications desirable in Regents, including character, cultivated minds, openmindedness, thoughtfulness, broadness of viewpoint, without prejudice, non-political in approach, capable of acting on the facts after deliberation and of reaching sound and objective conclusions, and deeply interested in building and maintaining in The University of Texas a University of the first class. Only Regents with these qualities can take over and discharge the responsibilities of governing the University in the present situation and go forward from this point to the achievement of the high goal of maintaining a University of the first class capable of leading the way in meeting the educational and spiritual needs of the people of Texas. Such a Board can be trusted to make a wise selection of a President from all available persons.

Present and voting for the statement:

Fred W. Adams	W. W. Hawkins
Hines H. Baker	H. R. F. Holland
Dr. E. W. Bertner	Dr. A. M. McAfee
Robert Lee Bobbitt	H. C. Pipkin
C. J. Cartwright	Walter S. Pope
L. H. Cullum	L. V. Stockard
W. H. Francis	B. D. Tarlton

Not present, but requesting that their names be added:

Dr. H. W. Harper	R. O. Kenley, Jr.
Judge J. C. Hutcheson, Jr.	W. H. Richardson, Jr.
E. James Kazen	Roger F. Robinson

After the reading of the statement, Mr. Francis continued: Now, that action or statement has been mailed to all the local student associations throughout the State; they are considering it and so far as I know now, no local association has turned it down. All that I know of or have heard from have endorsed it, some of them by unanimous vote; in one instance, at Dallas [it was] endorsed by a vote of 77 to 27 after a hot meeting of some two hours. It seemed to be principally between the medical alumni and the academic alumni, but at any rate by a majority vote it was adopted by the Ex-Students' Association at Dallas. The further it's gone the more I'm convinced, and I believe the Council is, that it is the basis for a fair solution of everything concerning what has happened in the past and presents a sound plan to go ahead with the University, to have a University of the first class. In other words, it does seem that it takes a new Board free from all of the matters which have heretofore transpired so that whatever they may do, the University and the Ex-Students in the State will have confidence in the decisions made and that right decisions will be made. As I view it, you can't settle issues between factions by the same men who created them as long as they function; even if their decisions might be right, they will not be accepted as judicial and as fair because it has come from minds that are already made up as to what they are going to do before they proceed.

It should be noted that the Regents never made a public answer to my charges. Regent Orville Bullington, however, did, as he said, reserve the right to make public the "reasons for his vote" to remove the President of the university. He did this in a lengthy prepared statement which he made public for the first time in his testimony before the Senate Investigating Committee. His statements were also endorsed by Regents Strickland, Schreiner and Stark. Since this statement had the endorsement of four members of the Board of Regents, it is the nearest thing we have to an "official" Regents' point of view of the controversy. It is desirable, therefore, to quote in its entirety in this study of the case:

REASONS FOR MY VOTE
Orville Bullington

At a regular meeting in Houston, on November 1, 1944, by a vote of six to two, the Board of Regents of The University of Texas removed

Dr. Homer P. Rainey from the office of President of the University. Following the meeting none of the Regents voting for Dr. Rainey's removal announced the reasons for their action. However, when I voted I reserved the right to state and place in the Minutes of the Board the reasons for my vote.

The University of Texas is the people's University. It stands at the head of our great system of public education in Texas, and its Board of Regents are the Trustees and representatives of all the people. The welfare of The University of Texas is the concern of all the people. They are vitally interested in the scholarship and character of its faculty. They require the highest standards for those who are to teach the youth of Texas. Those who tax themselves to support the University do so only because they expect its students to become better citizens for having had its training.

A Regent, therefore, should exercise the highest degree of care in discharging the important duties of his office. The fact that the office is one of trust and not of profit does not diminish the responsibility. It increases it.

The Regents who voted to remove Dr. Rainey did so because they believed his removal was absolutely essential to the welfare and future progress of the University. They acted only after the most careful and earnest consideration of all the questions involved. They knew that serious incidents which have happened would happen. They are prepared to accept and do accept full responsibility for the results of their action.

Many friends of the University wished to avoid the crisis which was certain to result from removing a President from office, and they suggested that some sort of compromise be effected. This could and should have been done if personalities and trivialities were involved. Those having good intentions can always afford to forgive and forget personal attacks and personal differences. Here, however, personalities were not involved. Here we are concerned with principles which are so axiomatic in their truth, and so fundamental in their character as to make compromise or appeasement unthinkable. Appeasement should never be made by sacrificing principle. Peace and tranquility bought at such a price is far too expensive.

We have great respect for those whose affection for the University moved them to offer their services in an attempt to compose the differences existing. We believe, however, that if they knew all the facts as we know them, they would have reached the same conclusion we reached. To understand some of the principles involved, it is necessary to give a brief summary of the duties and responsibilities imposed by law upon a Regent of The University of Texas.

Each Regent is a constitutional officer of the State of Texas, and must take an oath to perform faithfully and to the best of his ability the duties of the office, in accordance with the constitution and the laws. The duties of the Board are defined by statutes. It is required to "establish departments, determine the officers and professorships of the University," appoint persons to fill all positions it creates, prescribe their duties, fix their salaries, regulate the courses of instruction, and with the advice of the faculty prescribe the books and authorities to be used in the several departments. The Board is charged with the responsibility of conducting all the business affairs of the University and authorizing and ordering all expenditures.

During the first twelve years of its existence the University did not even have a President. However, the rapid growth of the University made it impossible for the Board of Regents to adequately direct its affairs without appointing a President and other officers to assist the Board in performing the many and varied duties imposed. As the University has grown it has been found necessary for the Board to delegate more and more of its statutory duties to administrative officers and assistants, but always their acts have been subject to the Board's approval.

The Board has sustained and defeated many attacks upon its authority and independence which came from without, but the Board was never called upon to repel such an attack from within, until October 12, 1944, when some of its appointees, led by Dr. Homer Price Rainey, President of the University, launched an unexpected and unprovoked attack upon it.

On more than one occasion when the Board refused to adopt President Rainey's recommendations, he threatened to publicly attack the Board and, as he expressed it, "take his case to the people." The Board of Regents overlooked this attitude, hoping that when his anger subsided he would think differently and forego such a course. It was our hope that he would finally learn to tolerate the opinions of the Board when it disagreed with him, and cooperate with it toward the development of a greater University. Our hope was in vain.

On October 12, 1944, President Rainey read a statement to the faculty and released it to the Press. This statement contained sixteen criticisms of the Board, or of some of its individual members. The first four of the sixteen actions of which he complains occurred before I or a majority of the Board became Regents; two of the four Regents criticized are no longer living. I became a Regent in January, 1941. Five of the Regents present at the Houston meeting have been on the Board less than four years, and during that time the Board has disagreed with the President on very few of the thousands of items which have come up for approval.

The Board of Regents is and should be responsible for any action taken by a majority of those present. The Board does not control the opinions of its individual members, nor can it discipline a Regent for his individual acts. The Governor can neither control nor remove a Regent. They can be removed by the Senate only after impeachment for malfeasance in office.

When Dr. Rainey issued a statement to the Press on October 7, 1944, to the effect that one of the nine Regents had "ordered" him to discontinue making religious addresses, and again referred to the same matter in his statement to the faculty, President Rainey knew that no such order had been authorized by the Board of Regents, because he was present throughout the Board's sessions at Austin on September 20th and 30th. He knew that no order from any individual Regent is valid and binding on the Board. He knew also that the Board acts only through the vote of a majority of those present at a meeting.

In this statement, therefore, it is proper that I refer only to those criticisms which involve me, an which involve the acts of the Board as a whole.

Complaint is made that the Board refused to reemploy three instructors in economics. This is true. These men went to Dallas to attend a meeting of citizens. The evidence showed that they later issued the following statement attacking the motives and good faith of those participating in the meeting:

"In connection with the allegedly spontaneous 'mass meeting held in FPA (Fair Park Auditorium) Sunday, we should like to make the following comments:

1. The meeting was not spontaneous—but was very organized.
2. The meeting was not democratically conducted—but all volunteer speakers were refused.
3. Speakers were not selected on the basis of representation —but on the basis of previously assured viewpoint.
4. The pretended fairness at the meeting was smoothly circumvented—condemning all sides in general and labor in particular."

A hearing was had because of complaints which were made by the citizens of Dallas and elsewhere, and the Board of Regents voted unanimously that these instructors had violated Section 6 of the University's rules and regulations. This rule, written by the late beloved President H. Y. Benedict, and adopted by a former Board, and accepted without change by this Board, provides:

"A member of the teaching staff is free to express, inside or outside the class room, his opinion on any matter that falls within the field of knowledge he is employed to teach and to study, subject only to those restrictions that are imposed by high professional ethics, fairmindedness, common sense, accurate expression, *and a generous respect for the rights, feelings and opinions of others.*"

The Board of Regents told the three economics instructors that their actions and their public statement showed a lack of proper respect for the rights and feelings of those participating in the meeting, including Dr. Umphrey Lee, President of Southern Methodist University, one of the speakers, and the late Dr. George W. Truett, who delivered the invocation. The instructors rejected the Board's proposal that they make some proper gentlemanly statement to the effect that they did not intend to show disrespect for the rights, feelings and opinions of those at the meeting. Whereupon the Board did not re-employ them.

In this course the Board did not restrain academic freedom. The discourteous and disrespectful conduct of these instructors, in my judgment, went far beyond the bounds of propriety, as well as academic freedom.

Complaint No. 6 is that the Board violated the principle of academic freedom in eliminating a novel entitled "U.S.A." as a required course of reading for Sophomores. The Board took this action after parents complained to members of the Board that the book was indecent, vulgar and filthy, and unfit to be made a required course in English for boys and girls. Board members examined copies of "U.S.A." and found that it contained much profanity, vulgarity, and was profusely interspersed with foul and obscene sex stories and blasphemous expressions. After its examination the Board ordered the immediate removal of the novel from the list of books required to be read, because it *was* unfit for required reading by young students. I particularly request the ministers and mothers of Texas to examine this book, and decide for themselves whether Dr. Rainey was right in commending this book, or the Regents were right in condemning it. The Board of Regents stands for decency in education, and I believe the overwhelming majority of Texans do.

Complaint No. 8 is that the Board does not favor tenure for faculty members, which I emphatically and unequivocally deny. The Board last year unanimously adopted the present excellent tenure rule. It is a tenet of recognized importance to the University and the individuals affected.

This rule was adopted after long deliberation by a joint committee of Board members and faculty members; the latter being Dr. J. W. Calhoun, former acting President of the University; Dr. Eugene C. Barker, eminent scholar and historian, and Judge Robert W. Stayton, a distinguished lawyer, judge and law professor. All three faculty members approved the rule as being more favorable in its wording to the interest of the University than the former rule which it supplanted, and they unanimously recommended its adoption to the Board. It provides:

> The Board desires to maintain, commensurate with the ideals of a University of the first class, a learned faculty, who, by precept and example, will inspire and instruct the students. To that end, competent teachers are given assurance that they may feel secure and independent in their position and that they will be promoted upon the basis of merit as circumstances permit.
>
> Termination of the employment of a professor or an associate professor or any other teacher before expiration of the stated period of employment, except by resignation or retirement for age in accordance with the rules, should be only for good cause shown. In each case the issue will be determined by an equitable procedure, affording protection to the rights of the individual and to the interest of the University.

This rule does not guarantee permanent, lifetime employment. The Regents have no such power. But it does declare a policy describing safeguards and procedure for the faculty.

It is significant that before the Board of Regents unanimously adopted the above tenure rule, the joint committee of the Regents and faculty members recommended the tenure rule quoted above, in the following language:

> It appeared to the Board of Regents that some revision of the language in the Rule of Tenure was necessary to avoid potential ambiguity. The Board requested the assistance of a faculty committee, and the revised rule is the result of the co-operation of a joint committee of the Regents and the faculty.
>
> The new statement has the unanimous approval of the members of the faculty committee consisting of Professors Calhoun, Stayton and Barker. It is the opinion of the joint committee that the wording of the new rule is more favorable to the interest of the University than that of the old rule.

Dr. Rainey also congratulated the joint committee and the Board for their action in adopting the tenure rule quoted, and later, so I am informed, wrote the members of the faculty committee expressing his approval of the tenure rule, and, although he had congratulated the Board for its action in adopting the rule, he added in his letter to the faculty committee the statement that "they had saved the faculty."

In his ninth criticism the President complains of the Board's curtailment of the expense of the Public Relations Department, particularly of the transfer of Dr. A. L. Brandon from the position of Director at a salary of $6,000 a year to an associate professorship of journalism. This action, as shown by the resolutions adopted, was taken as an economy measure by a vote of seven to one—Regent Harrison being absent. I moved the adoption of the resolution. The Board felt that more money was spent on public relations than the work of that department warranted. Many competent authorities believe that all state schools could well eliminate public relations expense, thereby saving the taxpayers of Texas about $200,000 annually. Last year the State Senate shared this view, voting to prohibit the spending of any money by state educational institutions for public relations. This provision, however, was eliminated from the appropriation bill in conference. Since 1941 the Board has reduced the cost of the Public Relations Department approximately two-thirds, without impairing its usefulness.

In his tenth complaint the President alleges that the Regents have shown a disposition to restrict freedom of research and thought in the University. He cites certain social science projects for which the Board refused to appropriate money. The Board favors research in all fields and has freely appropriated University funds for such purpose. The Board has no objection whatever to research work by professors, *on their own time and expense*, even on projects for which no appropriation is made by the Board. But the Regents are charged by law with the duty of selecting courses of study and expending the public funds for research projects, which, in their judgment, best serve the interests of the people of Texas and of the University. University funds for research are limited, and the Board had good reasons for utilizing the funds appropriated by the Legislature for other research projects than those complained of by the President. The few projects he mentioned are the only ones, as far as I can recall, out of several hundred presented to the Board during the past few years, for which it has refused appropriations.

Dr. Rainey is particularly critical of the Board's action at its last meeting, in refusing to appropriate $150.00 to finance a study of the effects of the Sacco-Vanzetti case upon American literature. Sacco and Vanzetti will be recalled as two immigrant Communists who were convicted of murder in Massachusetts several years ago and executed. The Board could not see how the study of literature could be advanced, or society benefited by the expenditure of the taxpayers' money on such a study. Incidentally, it is an interesting coincidence that the author of the novel "U.S.A." is mentioned in that book as a champion of these two Communist murderers.

The eleventh criticism made by Dr. Rainey is that the Board has refused to appropriate money from University funds for the establishment of a school of social work in the University, to train people in social case-work methods. The Legislature refused Dr. Rainey's request for such an appropriation, and the Board has felt that if the people's Legislative representatives were unwilling to vote the taxpayers' money for a social work school, we should not do so from other University funds. However, the Board has repeatedly stated that whenever the Legislature appropriated funds for such a school, the Board would have it installed. Meanwhile the Board intends to use the funds committed to it for purposes it deems more meritorious. For example, the Board believes that the faculty is underpaid, and one of its aims is to increase the salaries of the faculty rather than to create new departments; thus enlarging the teaching force and keeping the salary scale down.

In the twelfth complaint it is asserted that certain members of the Board objected to the Bureau of Municipal Research, and that only President Rainey's most urgent persuasion prevented its elimination. To the contrary, members of the Board have commended the work of this bureau. The Board has never even considered abolishing the Bureau; no motion was ever made, and no vote was ever taken on such a question, as the minutes will reflect.

Complaint No. 13 is that the Board adopted a resolution at its meeting on September 25, 1942, declaring the general policy of not allowing the use of University funds for payment of teachers' traveling expenses to meetings of National professional organizations of which they were members. The Board did adopt such a resolution. This was done in compliance with the Government's entreaties that civilian travel be limited to necessary trips during wartime congestion of transportaion. The Board expects to continue this policy as long as such conditions exist. However, the Board has not refused permission to any faculty member to go on such trips *at his own expense*, and it has paid, and will continue to pay the expenses of faculty members on trips that it considers are for the benefit of the University. This action of the Board has saved the University several thousand dollars annually.

The fourteenth point is a complaint that various differences have arisen between the President and the Board over legislative appropriations. This is the Board's first news of such differences. The complaint is that the University has never had adequate funds, and that the Regents urged the Legislature to cut the appropriation 22%, and the faculty to reduce the appropriation requests to the minimum.

During the last session of the Legislature many of its members joined with the Board of Control and the Governor in appeals to all Boards and State Departments to cut their budget requests to the utmost. Since the war had cut the number of University students almost in half, the Regents felt that some reduction could be made in the University appropriations without impairing its efficiency. However, the Board did not ask that the appropriation be cut. I do not know what statements individual members may have made to members of the Legislature. The Board, however, asked the Legislature to make the appropriation as large as it consistently could, with the understanding that the Board would save as much as possible and return all the savings to the treasury. The best evidence of the Board's ability to economize without impairing the University's functions is that during the fiscal year whch ended September 1st, the Board, after increasing salaries to meet increased living costs, has actually saved from its budget a minimum of $250,000 which will be returned to the state treasury and applied to the reduction of the deficit in the general fund. I do not believe the Board should be condemned for preventing the useless expenditure of public funds.

In the sixteenth complaint the statement is made that "the Medical School controversy, if written up in all its details, would provide a classic example in American higher education of how the Regents ought not to act." The Medical School controversy is written up in detail, to the extent of 2,175 typewritten pages of sworn testimony adduced by the Board in a hearing of nearly two weeks and taken down and transcribed by a court reporter, in May and June of 1942. This is a public record of the chaos wrought in that college while Dr. Spies was its Dean and Dr. Rainey was its chief executive. It is available for any interested person to read. The Regents were obliged to lose their time and to make this investigation when the Medical College was placed on probation by the Association of American Medical Colleges and by the Committee on Medical Education of the American Medical Association. These are the two national accrediting organizations on medical education. An overwhelming majority of the faculty petitioned the Board to remove Dr. Spies as Dean, and almost as many of the faculty requested the Board to no longer permit Dr. Rainey to have any connection with or supervision over the medical branch. The faculty represented to the Board that unless this action was taken tranquility could not be restored to the medical branch.

Dr. Rainey had had no previous experience in medical education before becoming President of the University, and the Board felt that he could be eliminated as chief executive of the medical branch without injury to the University. Accordingly the Board ordered Dr. Rainey to cease all supervision of the medical branch and leave the matter of working the medical branch out of its difficulty entirely to the Vice-President and Dean to be elected. At the request of Dr. Rainey this order was withheld from the minutes of the Board upon his promise not to further interfere in the affairs of the medical branch. At the same meeting, the former Dean was removed by the Board, and later Dr. Chauncey D. Leake, nationally prominent in medical educational circles, was elected Vice-President and Dean of the medical branch. The Board instructed Dr. Leake to take over the complete management and supervision of the medical branch, subject to the approval of the Board, and he has performed his duty since his appointment, reporting his recommendations and actions direct to the Board through the President. The results speak for themselves.

Turmoil and friction have ended. The College has been taken off probation by the two medical accrediting bodies. Many eminent medical educators have been added to the faculty. The Sealy-Smith Foundation has made a gift of $2,000,000 to the University to build a new modern hospital. A convalescent home for crippled children, valued between $150,00 and $200,000, has been given to the College by Mr. and Mrs. Maco Stewart; and $40,000 annually for five years has been made available to the College by the Buchanan Foundation for research in the cause and treatment of children's diseases. Standards in all departments of instruction have been raised and new departments added. More clinical material for medical education in the Galveston-Houston area will be provided as soon as hospital beds can be obtained. The Medical School now ranks among the top one-third of medical colleges in the United States, and the Board plans other additions and betterments to give it even higher standing, as soon as conditions permit.

The most important duty delegated and entrusted by the Board to the President is to select and recommend to the Board a faculty of the first class, without which there can never be a University of the first class. Too much care cannot be taken in investigating the character, scholarship, reputation and general fitness of persons who are to teach the youth of Texas, and mould and develop their qualities of mind and heart. Such care should be exercised regardless of the rank of the teacher to be chosen, for under our tenure rules, instructors become assistant professors, and then associate professors, and finally professors to hold for life or retirement, unless discharged for good cause.

Before one of our boys can secure a commission in the armed forces to fight the enemies of our country, they are each checked and double checked by the F.B.I. and other authorities as to scholarship, reputation, character and general fitness to become an officer.

Should the President of a great University be any less diligent in selecting those who are to mould the character and train the minds of the boys and girls who are to become our future citizens?

Recent developments have convinced the Board that President Rainey tragically failed to exercise proper care in discharging this most important trust committed to him by the Board. This conclusion was reached only when the Board learned that several teachers recommended by President Rainey were unworthy of their high profession. These have already resigned either voluntarily or by request. Two of these cases have had wide newspaper publicity, and I trust it will not be considered necessary to mention any of the others.

On October 12, 1944, the day President Rainey attacked the Board, there appeared in the *Dallas Times Herald* and other newspapers of the state the following article:

"University of Texas Professor Sentenced for Dodging Draft. Leavenworth, Kansas, October 12 (AP).

Arthur Goodwyn Billings, 33-year-old former instructor of economics at the University of Texas, was on his way to prison today at Terre Haute, Indiana. Billings will serve a two-year sentence imposed on a charge of refusing to submit for induction in the armed forces.

A onetime Socialist candidate for senator from Kansas, he left here yesterday for Terre Haute in the custody of a deputy U. S. Marshal. He had been held in the Leavenworth county jail since he pleaded guilty in U. S. District Court at Kansas City, Kansas."

The University was given further unfavorable publicity on account of Billings, and as late as November 6th the following article appeared in the newspapers:

"In Durance Vile, Kansas, Waits Votes. Topeka, Nov. 6 (AP) One of the candidates for high office in Kansas will spend election day Tuesday in his cell at Terre Haute, Ind. federal prison. He is Arthur Goodwyn Billings of Delphos, Socialist nominee for United States Senator.

Billings was sentenced recently to serve two years after he pleaded guilty to a charge of failing and refusing to report for army induction.

A former University of Texas faculty member, he was indicted and tried in federal court after winning a Supreme Court test of his contention that he was not under army jurisdiction because he had refused to take the induction oath."

During the winter of 1941 President Rainey learned that Billings claimed to be a "conscientious objector," but this information was not disclosed to the Board. Instructors are elected for one year only, but when the regular session of 1941-42 ended, and Billings' term as an instructor also ended, President Rainey, knowing that Billings objected to service in the armed forces of our country, again recommended him to the Board for a position as instructor in economics to take the place of one of the teachers not re-elected because of his conduct at Dallas, heretofore mentioned, and still President Rainey did not disclose the information which he had about Billings to the Board. The Board without any knowledge of Billings' subversive attitude re-elected him, relying upon Dr. Rainey's recommendation. Billings remained in the University as a teacher of economics until called for induction in the army in the latter part of August, 1942. He refused to take the oath of allegiance and did not enter the army. He was court-martialed and sent to prison. At the trial before a U. S. Judge in Kansas, reported in 46 Fed. Sup. 663, Billings claimed that he consulted various professors at the University about how to avoid induction in the army. He claimed he was a conscientious objector, but the court found he was not, but that he was in fact an agnostic. The court, in its judgment, found Billings to be a "perfect example" of "an over-educated, egotistical, scholastic slacker."

The court, after referring to the atrocities committed by Germany and Japan, said of Billings: "In the face of all these atrocities, this petitioner is one of the very few willing to violate the laws of his country and indirectly, at least, give aid and comfort to these world assassins. The petitioner says that Japan was justified (partly) in such treacherous attack."

Section 1, Chapter 2, of our Rules provides: "The President of the University shall . . . keep the Board fully and promptly informed and advised on all matters relating to the operations and welfare of the University. . . . The President shall recommend suitable persons to fill all vacancies and new positions . . . and give the Board information regarding the competency and diligence of officers, teachers and employees."

President Rainey knew, or ought to have known, that had he disclosed to the Board Billings' attitude toward defending our country in the present emergency, the Board would not have reemployed him. The Regents discussed with President Rainey reports which were being circulated during the summer and fall of 1942 to the effect that some University teachers had assumed unpatriotic attitudes toward the war efforts. These Regents were assured by Dr. Rainey that there was no truth in such reports and no cause for alarm. The evidence did not seem substantial enough to warrant any action by the Board, and none was taken. It is now known, however, that Billings was carrying on his subversive activities at the University during the summer of 1942, and it is known that he continued to do so until he was called for induction into the armed forces of the United States.

At the first meeting of the Board after the Regents learned about Billings' trial and conviction, Regent Strickland introduced a resolution for an oath of loyalty to be taken, and a questionnaire to be answered by all persons connected with the University in any capacity, including the Board of Regents. The motion did not receive a second, and the Board did not pass Regent Strickland's motion because it was thought that if any person connected with the University was in fact disloyal, they would be the first to sign up such an oath and questionnaire, and such procedure might be embarrassing to those whom the Regents knew to be loyal citizens, but I and other Regents believe that Regent Strickland was moved to introduce his resolution because of the publicity given the Billings case and we believe that he acted in good faith and within his rights, in his zeal to protect our country and the good name of the University and its faculty.

Within a few days of the time of President Rainey's attack on the Board, another shocking incident was reported in the Press. A University teacher, who had been recommended to the Board by President Rainey, and elected because the Board relied on the recommendation, was indicted by the grand jury of Travis County for an alleged unspeakable and unmentionable social crime.

Again, when the President in his statement attacking the Board not only approved the use of the book, "U.S.A." but showed that he had made no effort to ascertain the identity of the teacher responsible for making this book a required course of reading for students of tender age and was entirely out of sympathy with the action of the Board in the whole matter, the Board was deeply disappointed in the attitude of the President. When the Board barred the use of the book "U.S.A." as a required course of reading, it did not understand that President Rainey approved the use of this obscene and filthy volume, nor did its members have the remotest idea that he considered it one of the greatest books in American literature published in recent years. But now that he attacks the Board for suppressing the use of this book as a required course of reading for Sophomore boys and girls, after having nearly two years in which to read the book and carefully weigh the consequences of his decision, I am so profoundly and deeply concerned and disappointed in his attitude, that this alone, in my judgment, renders him unfit to be President of the University.

I have briefly stated the facts as to all actions taken by the Board of Regents, about which Dr. Rainey complains in his "sixteen point" statement of October 12th.

In his Point 16, however, he complained that Regent Harrison and I made a private and unannounced visit to the Medical College at Galveston in June, 1941. We did visit the Medical College at Galveston in our official capacity as Regents without consulting anyone, or asking their permission. Our visit, to the consternation of Dr. Spies and Dr. Rainey, was unexpected and unannounced.

Regent Harrison and I were the only new Regents appointed by the Governor in 1941. After we became Regents we found the Board closely divided on the question of retaining or discharging Dean Spies, because of a heated controversy existing between Spies and a majority of the faculty. We knew nothing about the facts, and did not even know of the controversy until we became Regents. We could not properly decide what was best for the medical college until we understood the facts. We thought it unwise to accept hearsay evidence from the Regents who were for or against Dean Spies. Accordingly we went to Galveston at our own expense to get the facts. We worked two days and got the facts. We found only one faculty member during our investigation that believed Dean Spies could ever work out the difficulties existing at the medical school. We concluded that the situation required a new Dean.

I returned home by Dallas and informed the then Chairman of the Board of our conclusion. Regent Harrison and I did not join in sending any ultimatum to Dr. Rainey to discharge Dean Spies. No ultimatum was sent to him by anybody. To the contrary, I suggested to the Chairman that rather than embarrass Dr. Rainey by having him make a recommendation that would be rejected, it would be an act of courtesy to inform Dr. Rainey that a majority of the Board opposed the re-election of Dean Spies. The Chairman agreed to the suggestion and later did so inform Dr. Rainey. Instead of accepting the suggestion in the spirit in which it was offered, Dr. Rainey angrily threatened to resign, and at the next meeting lengthily lectured the Regents opposed to Dean Spies' re-election on their functions as Regents, and criticized them for encroaching upon what he claimed was his prerogative as the President of the University. Later, all organized medical groups in Texas recommended that the Board give Dean Spies another opportunity. The Board accepted their recommendation. I would do so again if they or any other group of experts gave advice on a question with which I was unfamiliar. There was no pressure from these well known physicians. They presented arguments that we accepted. That is all. My attitude on the matter is disclosed in a statement which I filed in the Board's minutes of July 26, 1941. Other Regents joined in that statement. Although the Board at first stood six to three against the re-election of Dean Spies, the conclusion reached by Regent Harrison and me was later shown to be correct when the Board unanimously removed Dr. Spies as Dean, and this ended the trouble.

In his ninth criticism of the Board, Dr. Rainey complains of a conversation which I had with William McGill about becoming Director of the Public Relations Department. I did have such a conversation, but Dr. Rainey inadvertently failed to tell all that was said. Mr. McGill said he was not interested in the position because Dr. Rainey for some reason disliked him, and it would be impossible to pleasantly work with him.

I made the motion for reducing expenses of the Public Relations Department, and because Mr. McGill was already on the pay roll of the University, and the war had lessened his duties, I believed he could do the work he was doing and any which needed to be done in the Public Relations Department without any additional cost to the University. Dr. Rainey objected to Mr. McGill and said he could not work with him. He also objected to my motion, and claimed he had the right to name Dr. Brandon's successor under our rules. Regents Stark and Aynesworth agreed with the President but stated they would be glad to vote for my motion if it omitted naming Mr. McGill as Mr. Brandon's successor. I did not think then, nor do I now think, that our rules prevent the transfer of staff members from one duty to another except upon the President's recommendation, but I amended my motion by omitting Mr. McGill's name and providing that the vacancy when and if filled would be by a recommendation from the President. My motion carried 7 to 1. Dr. Brandon's work is being efficiently done by Miss Drummond, then his executive assistant. The annual expense of the Public Relations Department has been reduced about $20,000 since I became a Regent without impairing its proper functions.

In his statement of October 12th, as his reason or excuse for his attack on the Board of Regents, Dr. Rainey said:

"The whole matter boils down to two major issues. . . .

1. The issue of the freedom of the University. . . .
2. The issue of the recognition of the proper relationships between a governing Board and the executive and administrative officers of the University."

To prove his assertion that the freedom of the University is at stake, Dr. Rainey cites three acts of the Board as violating academic freedom and freedom of thought and research:

1. In his Point No. 5 he claims that the failure to re-elect three economics teachers who impugned the good faith and motives of those who attended a public meeting in Dallas early in 1942, including Dr. Umphrey Lee, President of Southern Methodist University, and the late Dr. George W. Truett, who delivered the invocation, violated the principles of academic freedom. All persons under all circumstances should be generous enough to respect the rights, feelings and opinions of others. A rule of the University requires this of all teachers. This principle is essential in a Democracy. The lack of it will destroy free government and make dictators of the majority. The three economics instructors disregarded the principles mentioned and the rule of the University which requires its observance. They refused to apologize for their conduct, and the Board refused to re-elect them to the faculty. Academic freedom is not involved here. No teacher in The University of Texas has academic or any other sort of freedom to gratuitously insult private citizens because of their opinions. Regents and faculty members are servants of the people of Texas—not their masters.

2. In Point No. 6 of his statement, Dr. Rainey claims that the act of the Board of Regents in suppressing the use of a novel called "U.S.A." as a required course of reading in English for Sophomore boys and girls, and all other classes, violates the principle of academic freedom. No teacher in The University of Texas or elsewhere should be permitted to teach immorality or obscenity to youths of tender age, or any other age. To prevent social pollution, the laws of our State and Nation forbid even the sending of immoral or obscene literature through the mails. Should the Regents and faculty members of the people's University be less diligent in protecting the character of the boys and girls committed to their care from such pollution?

3. In his Point No. 10 Dr. Rainey asserts the Regents have shown their disposition to restrict freedom of research in the area of social science. He names nine different projects, most of which had something to do with the Law Department. A majority of the Board are ex-students of the Law Department. We could view each of these projects dealing with the law with some degree of competency, and we did not think the results of this research would be worth what it was proposed to spend. This is no denial of academic freedom, but simply the exercise of judgment as to how to get the best results from the money to be spent on research.

These are all instances cited by President Rainey to prove his assertions that the Board of Regents oppose and interfere with academic freedom. Neither I nor any other Board member opposes academic freedom, and we have not denied it in any case. We are opposed to academic license. We know that for every right there is a corresponding duty, and for every freedom there is a corresponding responsibility. There can be no freedom, academic or otherwise, without assuming responsibility respecting the rights of others, and living by orderly processes.

The Board has not failed to recognize the proper relationships between it and President Rainey. The best evidence of this is that after six years as President he is able to find only sixteen points or instances wherein the Board has differed from his recommendations. Members of the Board, with only one or two exceptions, have had considerable experience as employees, as members of civic and business governing boards, and as executives. We think we know what is and what is not interference with the functions of an executive. We have in all our relations with Dr. Rainey observed the well-known customs and practices that exist between a governing board and an executive appointee. Dr. Rainey apparently is the one who does not observe these practices. He has a responsibility as the hired executive of the Board of Regents. If he was not satisfied with the policies of the Board and its actions generally, and did not want to cooperate with the Board, then he should have outlined his grievances to the Board instead of to the faculty and the Press, and then if the Board failed or refused to follow his suggestions, the only proper course for him to have pursued was to have resigned.

There is no more merit in the assertion that the Board opposed the tenure rule than in the assertion that the Board opposed academic freedom. The Board neither opposed academic freedom nor the tenure rule. I favor both of these rules, and I know that my views are shared by all members of the Board as constituted October 30, 1944.

It should be noted that all except three of the sixteen acts of the Board concerning which Dr. Rainey is critical happened more than a year ago. These three he says occurred at the September 1944 meeting or afterward. They are:

1. The Board refused an appropriation to investigate the effects of the Sacco-Vanzetti murder cases on American literature.

2. The Board refused to follow his recommendation to move the medical and dental colleges to Austin.

3. To quote Dr. Rainey [there was] "an effort on the part of one or more members of the Board of Regents to set limitations upon my activities, and the attempt to restrict the freedom of the President of the University." The Board took the first two actions named, but not the last. I joined with the whole Board at Houston in denying this last charge. I now repeat that denial. I never heard any Regent, either in or out of a Board meeting, discuss or mention restricting Dr. Rainey in making religious addresses. On the contrary, at our last meeting in Galveston I and others of the Board commended him for making such addresses. Dr. Rainey admitted this at Houston on November 1st. I do not believe he will deny it now.

Why then did Dr. Rainey attack the Board of Regents? Was it because it could not conscientiously spend public funds committed to it to glorify the Communist murderers? Surely not. Did Dr. Rainey attack the Board because of the policy it announced opposing the removal of the Medical College, thus abandoning a hospital gift of $2,000,000 and an endowment of ten or more millions for its support, and junking a plant carried on the University books at $4,600,000 besides making necessary the expenditure of several more millions to build a new medical school plant? Surely this policy-making act of the Board did not cause the attack, for Dr. Rainey in his statement concedes that the Board should decide the policies of the University.

Was the attack made on the Board because of statements said to have been made in a telephone conversation between the Vice-President and one Regent? It is unthinkable that Dr. Rainey would have attacked the Board and thus brought about the chaotic conditions in the University which have existed since, even if he thought one or more Regents wanted to do the things he says. All of the Regents were at home or returning home. In a few hours at the most he could have contacted every one of them and learned that they did not favor any of the restrictions or limitations he mentions. He did not contact one of the Regents, but on October 7th, a week later, a sensational interview, calculated to discredit the Board with the people, the students, and the faculty was given, and followed up on October 12th by his lengthy attack on the Board, read to the faculty and released to the Press.

Since it is improbable, if not impossible that either or all three of the matters above mentioned could either have inspired or caused Dr. Rainey's attack on the Board, and all the other incidents mentioned in his statement occurred from one to five years before these unwarranted attacks were made, the question still unanswered is, why did Dr. Rainey make these attacks on the Board of Regents, which he must have known would plunge the University into an ocean of confusion? Echo answers, Why? Why? Why?

Although much of President Rainey's 27-page statement relates to trivialities and personalities, which should have been and which I and other Regents thought were settled and composed long ago, there are fundamental principles involved which cannot be abandoned and upon which no compromise can be made. Among these are:

1. The Board may delegate to administrative officers statutory duties imposed upon it, but may not abandon its duty to supervise the manner in which such duties are performed by those to whom they are delegated.

2. Neither The University of Texas, nor any other educational institution supported by public funds secured by taxation, should be made subject to the will of one man, whose acts are free from any supervision or control by representatives of the people who provide the funds.

3. It is a duty of the Board of Regents, which may not be abandoned, to apply and interpret all rules adopted for the government of the University.

4. Members of the Board of Regents cannot without violating their oaths of office permit persons, groups of persons, or organizations to dictate opinions, acts and policies for the Board which are contrary to the judgment of the members of the Board.

5. Whether in or out of the classrooms, no member of the faculty of any educational institution, public or otherwise, has academic or any other sort of freedom, to violate the law, or to fail or refuse to observe generally accepted standards of courtesy, morality and common decency.

Neither the Board nor any of its members, to my knowledge, have either issued or inspired, directly or indirectly, any public attack on President Rainey, but as early as the commencement of 1943, if not before, Dr. Rainey indulged in public criticism of the Board. I make no attack on Dr. Rainey now. I am content to calmly, judiciously, and as briefly as possible, state the facts surrounding the transactions of which he complains. I have announced some of the fundamental principles which have guided the Board in the actions it has taken.

There can be little doubt that powerful forces in and outside of Texas have inspired and are directing this attack upon the freedom and independence of the University, and the right of the people to guide and direct and develop it into a University of the first class, through their own lawfully chosen Trustees and Representatives, the Board of Regents.

The attack may succeed. It will succeed unless its loyal and devoted friends among the people, the ex-students, the faculty, and the students come to the rescue.

I am physically unable to make the sustained and strenuous effort which will be necessary if the University is to be saved from those who would destroy its usefulness. As long as I can be helpful I am willing to expend what energy I have. Thousands of stout-hearted Texans have spent a lifetime defending the University and its Regents from attacks from without. I call on them to make one more effort to defend the University from this attack which comes from within, but which apparently is inspired and directed by forces from without.

Many fine friends of the University have been confused because no statement has been issued by the Board or any Regent. When I cast my vote I stated that I desired to prepare and file a statement of the facts and the reasons for my vote. When they have understood and carefully considered the facts and the principles involved, and the consequences to the welfare of the University, I am content to rely on the calm and deliberate judgment of the faculty, the students, the ex-students and the people, who are the ones most concerned.

The Regents, with one exception, are all ex-students of the University. They have spent much of their energies over the years in its service. They love the University with the same devotion and loyalty as the students, the faculty, the ex-students and friends of the University.

This crisis will pass as other crises have passed, with right triumphant, if the facts and issues are properly understood. The University is greater than any one man. It is greater than any group or organization of men. The Regents acted with, and have a firm and steadfast belief in, the necessity, righteousness and justice of their decision. They obeyed their oaths of office. They are confident that only good can come to the University if their action is sustained.

I am authorized to state that Regents H. J. Lutcher Stark, D. F. Strickland, and W. Scott Schreiner join me in this statement.

(Signed) Orville Bullington
Wichita Falls, Texas

MY
REBUTTAL

A number of statements and charges made by the Regents through Mr. Bullington's statement call for discussion and rebuttal.

One course of defense which I found particularly irritating was the repeated assertion by the Regents that they were only trying to carry out their obligations and responsibilities under the law. The implication through this assertion was that approval of my policies would require them to violate the law.

As a matter of fact, the laws of Texas relating to the Regents' control are so broad and so general that the Regents could meet every standard of a first-class university without ever coming close to a violation of the law or their oaths of office. Other Boards of Regents had met these standards before them, and Boards in other states had done it and were continuing to do it. I did not ask at any time for the change of a single law or Regent rule that was in effect when I became President of the university. There was nothing wrong with the laws or rules, and they had been in operation for many years. It was all a matter of attitude and policy on the part of this particular Board of Regents. The laws were so broad as to permit the Regents to run the university according to well recognized standards of great universities or to permit the Regents complete arbitrary control to run the university as they saw fit. They chose to run it the way they, and only they, saw fit. I was extremely disturbed by this, and I asserted under oath in the Senate that from the standpoint of the faculty and its rights of academic freedom every single measure that was initiated by the Regents (with one possible exception) was a restrictive or repressive measure. This Board seemed bent on curbing the university as a whole and the department of economics in particular, most probably because that department tried to present more than one side of economic policies and labor practices and thereby placed interests represented by some Regents in an embarrassing position. Ultimately, disfavor fell on the President himself, because he championed the faculty's rights of inquiry and research into unpopular causes.

In spite of the strong differences between myself and the Board concerning what constituted good university administration, I tried to the best of my ability to carry out the policies that the Board enunciated. I felt as an administrator that while a matter was in the formative stage, while a policy was being worked out, I should freely advise the Board and discuss the matter with them, but after that was done I felt it my duty to carry out the policies which the Board elected to follow. I do not recall that at any time the Board questioned that I had failed to carry out a policy that they had worked out.

Perhaps it is at this point that I should reply to Mr. Bullington's description of the problems which arose in the administration of the medical school.

This controversy was not of my making. I inherited it upon becoming President of the University, and did everything within my ability to resolve it. We had made substantial progress toward its solution when Bullington and Harrison entered the Board of Regents. The best evidence of this was that the Legislature had given us a vast increase in appropriations; larger than anything the school had ever received.

At that time Texas had a very poor rating among the medical schools of the country. We had begun work on the problem, and a fine program for the medical school evolved. Not more than a week before the Regents intervened in July, 1941, the mayor of Galveston congratulated me upon what had been accomplished, and said that the people of Galveston were happy about the situation. We were ready to begin building a first class medical school in Galveston; but the small group who had controlled the medical school for many years were not happy, and they had not surrendered the fight. They still had a trump card to play. This card was played by the Regents in July 1941 and by Bullington. I feel it is the best example of regential interference and bungling in the annals of the University, which led from farce to tragedy. As Bullington quoted me in his statement, "It is a classic example of how Regents ought not to act."

I covered all the factors in the controversy in a special report made to the people of Texas, and the Legislative Investigating Committee. I am happy to stand upon my record with the medical school. All that I needed for success was support from the Regents which, unfortunately, was lacking.

The thesis that the President is the agent of the Board is correct, but it is not complete. The President is indeed the agent of the Board in that he is charged with the responsibility of carrying into effect the policies and rulings of the Board. However, the President is *also* the chief educational advisor to the Board, and in that capacity he is to help the Board study problems and needs and is to make recommendations to them concerning the formation of policies for the university. It is certainly within the duties and responsibilities of the President to advise the Board when he believes any policy or proposal is not in harmony with good educational practices, or in his judgment is not in the best interests of the university.

Regent Stark summarized the problem succinctly when he said in his testimony:

Now, all of this [controversy] stems from one fundamental thing. It isn't anything new. It started when Dr. Rainey came on the Board, came to the University as President. And simply stated, it's just this: The Board of Regents are appointed by the Governor, they are confirmed by the Senate, they take an oath of office in which they swear to uphold the statutes and the laws, and to swear they haven't fought a duel; what the duel has to do with it, I don't know. Those laws are very plain. We can read them; we know what they mean. Here and now I should like to adopt Orville Bullington's statement of the situation as he made it very lengthily today. I concur in every word he said, but those are just instances of the problem. On the other hand, Dr. Rainey came to the University thoroughly imbued wtih the idea of making a great university out of it, but Dr. Rainey *wanted to operate and still wants to operate under the generally accepted academic practices.* Well, now, those two things clash, that's where we got into trouble and that's where we will always get into trouble. That's the meat in the whole cocoanut.

Dr. Burdine, the university's vice-president, analyzed the issue in almost the same way:

I will give you my own personal opinion, based on very close observations. You gentlemen of the Committee can put down on one side, in one . . . column, the testimony of Dr. Rainey . . . giving his vision of what a University of the first class is and should be. I think it's a courageous vision. It's a vision that's based on confidence, on hope, on the fundamental tenets of Christianity and democracy. It is, in other words, a positive program and in it there is no fear . . . of ideas so long as reason is left free to combat the bad ones. Now, . . . I would put in [another] column the testimony of the Board of Regents who voted to dismiss him. And for the most part, I am not saying wholly, but for the most part, I feel that theirs is a negative program representing an attitude of fear and suspicion. Fear of ideas, [a fear] one idea will get lost, a fear of Dr. Rainey and me when we would make recommendations. I am not using fear in the usual physical sense; I want to make that clear. I mean a sort of suspicion of our acts.

As time went on, the same thing might be applied to the faculty. You can either look on a University, as I see it, as a positive thing with boundless possibilities for good or you can look on a University as a prospective cause of trouble. Let me say right here that I think perfectly honest people can be on either side. I don't mean to put this picture in any derogation of any individual or another. I think there can be honest people on either side and never is one side completely right or one side completely wrong. But it is, I think, a question of attitude, . . . and I think when you compare those two points of view, . . . that the choice that I made was really an easy choice to make in comparing these things. I think one represents a positive approach. The dictionary defines "positive" as an affirmative, constructive, as distinguished from, let us say, skeptical, and I think Dr. Rainey has had a very positive approach to the building of a University of the first class. I think the other, frankly, represents a *negative approach* to the problem of building a University of the first class. I think you could get two people side by side; one can have a positive approach, his confidence based on hope and faith, the other just as honest and a little bit afraid of the situation getting out of control or something of that character, and there will certainly be a great difference in the product that finally comes out.

So, in spite of Regent Bullington's statement the issue was not a question of running the university according to the laws; it was simply a question of *how* it was to run under the broad powers which the laws gave the Board. The tenure rule provided a good case in point, and Mr. Bullington's statement glosses over the facts.

The tenure rule had been part of the university policy for many years. It was satisfactory to the faculty, and it met all the requirements of the Southern Association and the A.A.U.P. Furthermore, all Boards of Regents in the past had operated happily under it. Why was there suddenly a need to change it? The Attorney General, at the Regents' request, ruled upon the tenure rule; he stated that the rule as it was drawn was perfectly good law and in no way interfered with the laws of Texas, and he ruled that the tenure rule did not constitute a contract for a permanent life-time position. So there was no valid reason for changing the rule. The plain fact is that the Board did not start out to change the tenure rule. They intended to *abolish* it. It was in their way. They had tried to fire men whom they disliked from the faculty, and the tenure rule required that a due process of law be followed—that firing could not be done on an arbitrary basis. The Regents over and over stated their intention to get rid of the rule. They only came around to a willingness to *change* the rule after the President, the faculty and the Ex-Student's Association had raised strong protests about it. It was only then that they receded and consented to work with a faculty committee to *revise* the rule, and when it was revised the Regents were able to incorporate a provision which made a real joker of the rule—a provision that the Board could declare "an emergency" when their own judgment approved and thus set aside the due process guaranteed the faculty under the old rule.

In order to try to make their revision of the rule more pleasing to the faculty they proposed to extend the provisions of their rule to cover the lower ranks in the faculty which were not included in the old rule.

The issue of Communism, too, was a smoke screen. There were no Communist teachers in the university. Criticism of certain teachers of economics had been going on for years, and they had been investigated time and time again, always with the same result: their views might be unpopular, but they were not Communistic. During the war we had been especially careful. The university joined the war effort, and was carrying on a large training program for the armed services. We had initiated a large Naval ROTC program, and the Navy made a thorough check on the university before this was done. The F.B.I. was there many times and kept a close check upon everything. Mr. Martin Dies also came and his investigator spent about two weeks on the campus. The administration gave him complete cooperation, and he found nothing disturbing to report. During the Senate investigation, Strickland admitted that not a single Communist had been discovered on the faculty or staff of the university. Mr. Bobbitt made the following comments upon this issue in his Senate testimony:

For instance, let me make an example, perhaps you remember—all of us do, I imagine—the tirade that went on about the school being full of Communism, and the rumors were something terrific. I personally knew that there wasn't a word of truth in it. I had three boys come out of this school and I had watched the student body; [there is] no student body in the world that's performed as nicely in the initiation and carrying on of the war as this student body. There were no demonstrations, no failures to perform in selective service and what have you, and yet some other universities in the United States had riots and refusals of the student body to do things. This demonstration of the student body in the present crisis is a magnificent compliment to this university and to the faculty and the administrative officers. As far as I know, there's been no window broken, no property destroyed, and yet it's been very tense so that somebody couldn't sit up and tell me that its full of Communism. And finally Martin Dies kept on circulating reports and Dr. Rainey told him to put up or shut up. He shut up and all the rumors stopped.

It wasn't Communism that the Regents were worried about; Communism simply provided an excuse. What they were really worried about was liberalism, by which is meant any teachings that were out of line with extreme conservatism. For example, any activities or teaching that was pro-labor was obnoxious to them. Any friendliness shown to Negroes, or any proposals to secure better educational opportunities for them, was considered to be radicalism; any support for civil liberties or any questioning of the operation of the economic system was heresy. These were the things that the Regents wanted to stop, but these issues were no longer the bugbears they once were, and in order to make them look vile, the labels of "socialism" and "Communism" had to be applied.

The Regents tried to make it appear that the four instructors who attended the Dallas meeting were discourteous and offensive, and did not show the proper respect for the feelings of others. These charges fell under the Regents' rules, but the instructors could not be tried for liberal attitudes under the rules. The Regents were subject to pressure on this matter from without the Board. One of the letters which Regent Bullington received from Mr. LeFevre, Jr. began by saying:

"The socialistic attitude exemplified by the four instructors in the Economics Department at The University of Texas and the President of the University is a dangerous situation."

This feeling also troubled Judge Davidson, who addressed a letter to the Board of Regents about the same incident. He said:

"It seems that we have a branch of our university swinging away from true economics and routing our children into the camp of state Socialism borrowed from totalitarian Europe."

The Judge therefore thought the Regents ought to "give serious consideration to the matter of making a wholesale change in the economics department of the University." In fact, he called for a housecleaning of the economics department. The Judge did not make any issue of discourtesy or lack of respect for anyone.

This opposition to the economics department is the key to much of the negativism of the Regents, and toward the university by the plutocracy in Texas. Most of the Regents belonged to that group and they were trying to bring the economics department in line with "true economics," as Judge Davidson had requested. To them the New Deal was wholly evil, and anyone who had any sympathy for it was a radical. Because I had been in Washington for four years prior to coming to the university, it was assumed by many people that I had been a bureaucrat. In actuality I had been Director of the American Youth Commission, which was sponsored by the American Council on Education and financed by the Rockefeller Foundation, but most people thought that I had been a part of the *National* Youth Administration. Consequently I was suspect, too, on that count. A member of the senate committee said to me, "I want to know what your connections were before you came to The University of Texas. I've heard it rumored that you were a radical New Dealer and hooked up with the New Deal set-up; I want to know what that connection was and just what you did before you came to The University of Texas."

However, my chief sin in the eyes of the plutocracy was "protecting these radicals" on the faculty by insisting upon freedom of teaching and their rights to fair dealings. I would not go along with any arbitrary dismissals, or, later on, any desire to change the Regents' rules so that the Regents would not be handicapped by them. By their actions, which I knew were contrary to the standards of all good universities, I was forced into the very undesirable position of having to take issue with my governing board, and sooner or later, of course, this had to lead to open conflict. The President is not protected by tenure rules; he is subject to the will of the Board and may be removed at any time they desire. In this case, the president was insisting upon fair play for the faculty and this was in the way and incurred the Regents' opposition.

It must be remembered that the group in Texas who wanted to get control of the university had been at work on this project for some time. The members of the Board who had elected me and who were favorable to my leadership had not been reappointed. These included Major J. R. Parten, who had become Chairman of the Board and who believed in sound principles as strongly as I did. He had a clear understanding of those principles and a full appreciation of what they meant to the development of the university. It is a pity that he could not have remained on the Board indefinitely. However, he did not belong to this group of ultra-conservative business leaders in Texas. He was an independent oil man; he had his own company and did not belong to one of the big national integrated companies, and the independent oil men in Texas were *persona non grata* to the big companies.

Furthermore, Mr. Parten was a liberal Democrat and believed that the policies of these other forces were destructive and were not in line with the best interests of the state and the nation. He loved The University of Texas and wanted to see it become one of the truly great universities of the nation, but he had worked for the New Deal in Washington, and of all things evil, he had been appointed by Mr. Harold Ickes who, to this group in Texas, was the personification of socialism and radicalism. Mr. Parten therefore had no place in their plans for bringing the university under control. He had demonstrated that he would not play politics with the university and would not permit others to do it if he could prevent it. He insisted that the university should be operated in harmony with sound educational practices, and he had carefully informed himself of what these standards were. He had taken a leading part in cleaning up a bad athletic situation and in bringing it more in line with the best interests of the university. He had made a careful study of the unhappy medical school situation in Galveston, and we were well on the way to a sound solution of that problem when he was not reappointed to the Board. He had also shown his definite support for the principles of freedom by his insistence upon following the rules and standards relating to them. He had a keen and independent mind; he did his own thinking, and would join in no combinations or political agreements of any sort. Having him dropped from the Board was an essential step in the plan to get control of the university.

Along with Mr. Parten went Dr. George Morgan of San Angelo, who also had a fine mind and a liberal spirit. He was a highly trained geologist with a Ph.D. degree in that field. He, too, knew what a great university should be and how it should be operated, but he, like Mr. Parten, was an independent oil man. So, he, too, did not belong in their camp for he did not conform to their patterns of thought and action, and he was replaced.

Another Regent who was not reappointed was Mr. Leslie Waggener, who was the son of the first President of The University of Texas. He was a man of high ideals and great personal integrity. He loved the university and was devoted to its welfare. However, he was in a very difficult position. He was a leading official in The Republic National Bank in Dallas, and, as such, he was under constant pressure from the big financial group centered in Dallas. He was also a very sensitive man—sensitive not only to the high ideals represented in his family background but also to his obligations as a leading bank official in a key economic center in Texas. He therefore very soon found himself caught between these two sets of forces.

One incident will illustrate Mr. Waggener's difficulties. Over quite a period of time the Board of Regents of the university was confronted with the issue of whether or not an honorary degree should be granted to Mr. Jesse Jones of Houston, who was at the time Chairman of the Reconstruction

Finance Corporation. The university had previously conferred such a degree upon Vice-President John Nance Garner, but after that the Board had decided that it was unwise for a state university to grant honorary degrees and had declared a policy against it, with which Mr. Waggener was in agreement. However, in spite of this announced policy, the question of a degree for Mr. Jones kept coming up in one way or another. It made a very difficult problem for the Regents and the Administration, since the President was thoroughly in harmony with the policy of not conferring honorary degrees. Mr. Waggener was in a peculiarly difficult spot, since Mr. Jones because of his position in Washington wielded a powerful influence over the banks of the country, and was probably the most powerful personality in Washington save President Roosevelt himself. Mr. Waggener, therefore, was most anxious that the issue should never come before the Board if it could be avoided, for if it did ever come up for a vote, he simply could not vote against it. He was also very anxious to see the President of the university stand firm in his support of the declared policy and to use his influence to prevent the matter from ever coming before the Board for definite action.

The medical school controversy was another issue that tore Mr. Waggener apart. He was a life-long friend and a great admirer of Dr. Edward Randall of Galveston, but as the controversy over the medical school developed he found himself again in great conflict between his personal feelings and friendship for Dr. Randall, and the sounder policies and interests of the university. This conflict was so intense within himself that he could find no way to resolve it without great personal distress, and ultimately this distress forced him to resign from the Board. His leaving the Board was a loss to the better interests of the university.

Mr. E. J. Blackert was a fourth member of the Board to be replaced. He was a member of the Board that employed me, and was helpful and cooperative with me as long as he remained upon the Board. Like the above-mentioned Regents, he was not in sympathy with the desires of this ultra-conservative group to limit and restrict freedom in the university.

Thus, one by one, the Board of Regents was changed, and

every change brought the Board further under the control of the reactionary economic and political forces of the state.

One argument used by the Regents in trying to refute some of the charges that I had made against them was that the Board is responsible for actions of the majority, but does not control the opinions of individual members. Hence, what individual members said to me or asked me to do did not represent "Board action," and I had no right to use them as criticisms against the Board.

This argument was clearly an evasion of responsibility. Individual approaches form a subtle, off-the-record method of putting pressure on the President, and cannot help but create tension between the administration and the Board. When the President is confronted with a direct request to take a specific action, he must either grant the request or deny it. He is forced into an uncomfortable position, and the more often this happens the more uncomfortable he becomes, and the greater the tension between him and the Board. Just because the request has come from an individual does not make that request meaningless. All of the individuals vote when the Board meets to discuss policies, and the President is always aware of how important it is to have a friendly Board.

Suppose that I had acceded to these individual requests. Suppose I had fired the Director of Athletics, had fired Dr. Montgomery from the economics department, and had dismissed the three men who displeased Mr. Stark. I was well aware of what the ensuing events would be. There would have been turmoil in the athletic department, just when a satisfactory situation there had been reached. There would have been extremely low faculty morale, and mistrust of me by the faculty. And in taking these actions, would I or would I not have been acting at the direction of the Board?

The Board insisted that I had no right to criticize it as a whole for what individuals had tried to persuade me to do. However, this individual approach was attempted so often, and by diverse members, that I could not but conclude that the Board as a whole was seeking by this method to pressure me into taking actions they as a Board recognized would be unpopular in some circles.

Mr. Parten strongly supported my position on this issue before the Senate Investigating Committee. He said that "often individual action of Regents is as damaging or more damaging to the University's welfare than are instances of collective action. . . . I assure you that my experience has shown that repercussions from acts of this kind can and do bear upon the disposition of more important institutional problems."

Notice should be taken of Regent Bullington's charge that "recent developments have convinced the Board that President Rainey tragically failed to exercise proper care in discharging this most important trust committed to him by the Board." He referred to the selection of faculty.

In support of this charge he mentioned two cases. One of these cases was that of Mr. Arthur Billings, who maintained he was a "conscientious objector" to war, and who was later sent to prison for refusal to be inducted into the army. Vice-President Burdine made the following statement about the Billings case before the Senate Committee:

Now, remember that Billings came in September 1941; it was past midwinter when the matter of his [conscientious objection] . . . was communicated to us by the Chairman of the Department. . . . The local Board put him in 1-A, and when you got in 1-A you would think that he would either be called or else passed on the conscientious objection soon. Well, the Board didn't do anything for several weeks and incidentally Billings was checked thoroughly by the proper governmental agencies. I talked with several of them about him and probably knew at that time whether an objection such as he had was a conscientious objection or not, and as soon as it was determined that it would not be, he was called by his Board and at that time his resignation was submitted. He is the only conscientious objector that I know of that we had on the faculty and we have got about seventy [faculty members] in the military services on leave at the present time."

This record does not support a charge of lack of diligence on anybody's part in the handling of the Billings case. Dr. Ralph Himstead in testifying before the Senate Committee said, "and I should like to say that Dr. Rainey handled the case of the conscientious objector admirably."

The other case which Regent Bullington used to support his charge of failure to exercise proper care in the selection of faculty was the case concerning homosexuality on the part of two faculty members. Mr. Bullington made these separate charges in connection with it: (1) that the President didn't press the case with enough vigor; (2) that the President was negligent in that he delayed informing the Regents for several months; and (3) that the President should have prevented their being on the staff in the first instance; that proper diligence on the President's part would have detected them when they applied for appointment.

The first two of these charges were adequately refuted by the testimony of Mr. Homer Garrison, who was Director of the Department of Public Safety in Texas. This department is charged by the Texas government with the detection of crime.

Mr. Garrison reviewed at length before the Senate investigating committee the steps that were taken to investigate all factors in this case. He emphasized that I had been completely cooperative with his department in its investigation. He was asked by Senator Lane: "I would like to know if after Dr. Rainey reported this to you, did he show any lack of diligence on his part in helping your department, to cooperate with your Department in trying to work this situation out?" Mr. Garrison replied: "No sir . . . He did cooperate. . . . He has never failed us that cooperation."

Regent Bullington's third charge that these men should have been detected as homosexuals at the time of their application is reduced to absurdity by his own inability to detect one after two hours of personal quizzing on his part—an incident he neglected to mention. When this matter was being discussed in the Board, members of the Board asked that we bring one of the men under investigation before the Board for their personal observation. This was done, and for a long time Regents Bickett and Bullington, both of whom were lawyers (Mr. Bullington had boasted of the fact that he had been a prosecuting attorney and was therefore not without experience in such matters), put this person through his paces. He stuck by his claim of innocence, and at the end of the quizzing Mr. Bullington said to him, "Well, I don't think you are guilty." About two weeks later this same man made a confession of guilt to one of the officers of the law. It is rather obvious that if these two experienced attorneys had the "suspect" before them for direct examination for two hours and couldn't detect guilt of the kind under consideration, there is no case against the authorities of the university who hired the man in the first place without any suspicions of guilt. The only conclusion which is justified is that this charge was not an honest or a sincere one, but was apparently an attempt to smear. It was an effort on Regent Bullington's part to try to derive political gain and moral advantage out of a very unhappy experience for the university.

Mr. Bullington's handling of the dispute concerning the novel *U.S.A.* had a similar ring of insincerity about it.

He made so much of this case that the Board of Regents held an all-day special meeting to investigate it. The Board called upon the department of English for an explanation of why this book was upon the reading list of a course in Sophomore English. The department made a full written report of the entire matter. This report said in part:

The President of the University was in no way responsible for the use of Dos Passos' *The Big Money*. Responsibility for its use in English 312Q during the first semester of the session 1942-1943 lies entirely with the Department of English. . . . Among teachers and critics of contemporary American literature, *The Big Money* is regarded as a serious, highly moral book, in both theme and treatment. Fundamentally it is a sermon on an old text, "The wages of sin is death." . . . The controversy resulting from the use of *The Big Money* has convinced us that its use in a Sophomore course was imprudent. . . . The committee in charge of English 312Q had already recognized objections to the use of *The Big Money* from within the faculty, and had voted to drop the book, before the Regents took action and before the Committee knew of any regential interest in the matter. The action of the Regents eliminated the book somewhat more promptly. They ordered it dropped immediately on January 9, whereas the Committee had recommended dropping it at the end of the semester and classes continued to January 22.

The Committee then added this significant statement:

But the action of the Regents gave the book, the Court, the Department and the Regents themselves a kind of publicity that the Committee wanted to avoid.

Actually the Regents' action made the book the most popular book in Texas, and within a short time it could not be found in any bookstore in the state.

The other position which the Regents tried so hard to defend was their action relative to the four instructors in the economics department who were discharged for their failure to respect the rights, opinions and feelings of others. Fortunately a stenographic report was made of the Regents' investigation of this case, which supplements the testimony of Professors Ayres, Hale and others before the senate committee. The A.A.U.P. also made a thorough investigation of this case, and Dr. Ralph Himstead said it was well handled. Some excerpts from the stenographic report of the Regents' hearing on the case of the four instructors will show the course the questioning took, and the nature of the replies.

Questions by Mr. Bullington:

Q. Do you agree to this statement: "A member of the teaching staff is free to express, inside or outside the classroom, his opinion on any matters that fall within the field of knowledge he is employed to teach and to study, subject only to those restrictions that are imperial by high professional ethics, fair-mindedness, common sense, accurate expression, and a generous respect for the rights, feelings, and opinions of others." Do you believe that?

A. Yes, sir.

Q. Do you think that you professors exhibited on the occasion in question a generous respect for the rights, feelings, and opinions of these speakers at this meeting when you charged that their meeting was not spontaneous, that it was an organized effort to smear the President, that it was not democratically conducted, that the speakers were not selected on the basis of representation, that its fairness was only pretended, and that all fairness was smoothly circumvented, and that it was for the purpose of condemning labor? Do you think that that exhibits a generous respect for the feelings and opinions of those people of this state who were meeting in mass meeting for the purpose of petitioning Congress to redress their grievances?

A. The mass meeting was for the purpose of considering the problem involved—not for the purpose of stating a pre-determined viewpoint.

Q. Regardless of what the mass meeting was for, do you think that you showed a generous respect for their feelings and opinions?

A. We did not criticize any of the speakers at any time, I can assure you.

Q. You charged there was no fairness in it?

A. We criticized the conduct of the meeting. As a matter of fact, I don't know yet who organized the meeting.

Q. You contacted Mr. Hoblitzelle—you knew that Mr. Hoblitzelle was Chairman?

A. Yes, sir.

Q. He was the man that you approached and asked to be allowed to speak?

A. Yes, sir.

Q. You knew that Mr. Hoblitzelle was Chairman of the meeting and was in charge of it. Do you think that after a meeting is held that you should go out and give a statement such as that to the press, or that you should go to Dallas and issue any kind of a statement regardless of what your views are on the 40-hour-a-week business? I am interested in impressing on you that the members of the staff are servants of the people, and not their masters. Do you think that you are showing a generous respect for their feelings and their opinions and rights when you issue such a statement as that?

A. Yes, sir; I do.

Q. You knew at the time that regardless of which side you are on about the 40-hour week, you knew that was a political controversy, didn't you?

A. I should think it was much more than that.

Q. There was a political controversy raging at that time in Congress, and there was an amendment in Congress at that time which was being discussed all over the country, and it was being discussed all over the country as a political measure, wasn't it?

A. That is right.

Q. For you to leave your duties here and go to another city where a meeting was being held, regardless of the purpose, and issue a critical statement, do you think that you complied with Rule 6, which says that "a member of the staff should refrain from expressing personal opinions that might, because of the University connections, incorrectly be thought to be within his special field of knowledge." Now, do you think you absolutely refrained from getting into that controversy?

A. Not a harmful one.

Q. You do admit that that was a question of partisan politics?

A. It is owing to what you mean by partisan politics, isn't it?

A. If you define political question as anything upon which people take sides or a bunch of people disagree, then, it is impossible to teach anything in the social sciences.

Q. I am talking about involving the University and yourself. Why did you tell them that you were from the University?

A. I would hate to lie to them about it.

Q. Couldn't you have refused to answer questions as to where you were from?

A. I guess so.

Q. And not involve the University at all?

A. I did not think anyone would suppose that was the University's opinion.

Questions by Mr. Bullington:

Q. Did you ever labor any with your hands?

A. Well, I was carry-out boy in a grocery store when I was younger.

Q. You never chopped wood or picked cotton on a farm?

A. No.

Q. You never punched cattle any?

A. No.

Q. Your labor ideas are largely theoretical, and not practical—not being from practical experience?

Questions by Judge Strickland:

Q. Do you approve of sit-down strikes that were conducted by the C.I.O.'s? Do you think that was a good legitimate practice?

A. Oh, I have never made any statement.

Q. Were you for or against it?

A. I would want to think about it.

Q. You believe it is a good rule for the C.I.O.'s to require industry to take out of the payrolls of the people their labor dues and deliver them to the C.I.O.?

A. That is not what is at stake here.

Q. I just want to know whether you think that is a good practice?

A. The deduction of C.I.O.s' dues may be.

Q. The deduction of dues from the payrolls by the companies? That is what Lewis requires them to do?

A. If the union and the employer agree to that, that is up to them.

Q. You still have no idea whether sit-down strikes are a good or a bad thing?

A. No.

Q. What would you tell your class about that?

A. I have talked about the sit-down strikes, and what I usually say is to describe it and to conclude the discussion by saying the Supreme Court has declared it constitutional.

Q. You have no personal views as to whether the sit-down strike is just or unjust?

A. I have not formulated any idea specifically. I have never made a specific study of sit-down strikes.

Questions by Dr. Aynesworth:

Q. Do you believe in the principles of American democracy that were founded by our forefathers and practiced by our immediate ancestors and ourselves?

A. Oh, I certainly think I can say that without question, although I realize one can quibble over specific things that are changing or that are at stake, but certainly I am profoundly a democrat.

Questions by Judge Bickett:

Q. What principles do you think are changing?

A. Oh, things like the sit-down strikes come up and are issues and are resolved one way or the other. As I say, I have not formulated any ideas specifically how that should come out. Those issues arise from day to day.

Q. I thought you said some principles are changing?

A. Some elements in the situation.

Questions by Mr. Bullington:

Q. Do you believe in the doctrine of production for use?

A. All production is for goods to be used.

Q. I am talking about doctrine of production for use that Upton Sinclair had up in California?

A. I think you probably refer to a talk that was reported in the *Daily Texan*.

Q. I am asking you if you believe in this doctrine of production for use only, and not for profit?

A. I don't think that term has any specific technical meaning.

Q. You think that production is for use, and not profit?

A. You mean, do I mean the abolition of the profit system?

Q. Yes.

A. No.

Q. What is an "economic royalist"? What is your conception of an economic royalist?

A. Well, I might say in the jargon of economics, I don't think there is any precise definition of that.

Q. In your mind what do you consider an economic royalist?

A. I would say that Mr. Morgan, and Mr. Rockefeller, was an economic royalist.

Q. What characteristics and prerequisites are necessary before one becomes an economic royalist in your mind?

A. I am not capable on the spur of the moment to give you a hard and fast definition.

Q. What do you think to be one?

A. I hesitate to say.

Q. You would not know what an economic royalist is?

A. As a precise definition, no.

Q. Could you approximate it?

A. By examples I could.

Q. I might want to try to keep from being an economic royalist, if it is a bad thing to be one. On the other hand if it is a good thing to be one, I might want to be one. What is an economic royalist, if you know? What do you mean by that when you use the term "economic royalist"?

A. Oh, certainly, economic royalists would have some of the characteristics of their set-up. They would be in position, as a result of their wealth, and their position in the economic world, to have a considerable and very marked influence on the course of economic events, certainly. I doubt if that definition would rule out everybody that is not, and include everybody that is, perhaps.

Q. The reason I ask that question [is that] I see here in this paper that Dr. Gordon bitterly attacked the economic royalists. That is the reason I thought you might know who they were. You say, "Economic royalists who starve the masses for their own profit." I wondered what principle you were attacking.

A. When you brought this up I asked you if this was the speech you referred to as I wanted to say in that connection that I had not in that speech used the expression "economic royalists."

Q. You did not use that term "economic royalists"?

A. I don't think so.

Q. You did not attack any economic royalists?

A. I will be glad to give you a copy of that speech, if you wish to see it.

Q. Was it a written speech?

A. Yes.

Q. I would like to see it. You did not depart from the text in making it?

A. No, sir.

Q. That ought to solve a lot of problems then. By the way, what was the subject of your thesis for your Master's degree?

A. The subject of my Master's thesis was "The Foreign Policy of Argentina," and the subject of my Doctor's thesis was "Expropriation of Foreign Owned Property in Mexico."

Q. Were you for that or against it?

A. I can safely say, I think, that there is no for or against—that there is no black or white in that issue.

Mr. Bullington: That is all.

I have quoted this questioning by the Regents at length, for I believe it reveals the attitudes of the Regents better than any other document that I could present. It is hardly necessary to point out that the questioning in this investigation varied widely from the topic supposedly under investigation.

When the issue of the three economics instructors arose, I, as President, asked the economics department to make a full investigation of the case. This was done and this report exonerated the instructors and concluded that they had not violated any university rules and that their conduct had not been improper. Professor C. E. Ayres, in his testimony before the Senate Investigating Committee, stressed these points. He said in part:

These three instructors attended that meeting as spectators and never even raised their hands to try to attract attention. They had been told in advance that they would not be permitted to speak out and they made no effort to speak. They did not interrupt the meeting. They did not cause any disturbance, and any suggestion to that effect is defamatory.

One of the charges against the Regents' control of the university, and also of the entire educational system in Texas at this time, was that this control had fallen into the hands of a group of men who represented a solid conservative social, political, and economic philosophy, and that this control was the direct result of political planning under the regimes of Governors O'Daniel and Stevenson. This charge appeared in many places—in newspaper editorials, and especially in the testimonies of Major Parten, Robert Bobbitt and J. Frank Dobie before the Senate investigating committee.

Regent Bullington vigorously denied and ridiculed any idea of interlocking economic interests on the various boards of state institutions, but the testimonies of Messrs. Parten, Bobbit and Dobie stated facts to the contrary. Major Parten, who was Chairman of the Board of Regents in 1940, testified before the Senate Investigating Committee as follows:

I feel it is my duty as a citizen and as a former student of the University to relate to you that it is my considered opinion that certain definite political activity was started about the year 1940 which had as its purpose the influencing of governing board appointments so as to eliminate from our institutions of higher learning so-called radical teachers.

He followed this statement by citing a number of cases that came to his attention as Chairman of the Board. He said:

I received literally dozens of complaints averse to the retention of Dr. Robert Montgomery on the Economics staff . . . and there were others.

He referred to the charge of Congressman Martin Dies that there was Communistic activity at the university. He cited the case of Regent Bronson's efforts to remove Dr. Montgomery from the faculty by making a motion in the Board to strike his salary from the budget for the year 1940-41. He said further:

About the middle of the summer of 1940 . . . I had a conversation with a prominent Texas attorney who came to my Houston office to tell me of his attendance at a meeting of several business executives and attorneys whose declared purpose was to influence educational board appointments of men who could be counted upon to eliminate from the teaching staffs in higher education of Texas all radical elements in the faculties.

Mr. Bobbitt's contribution to this issue was made before the Senate committee in these words:

> Reference has been made in the testimony here to interlocking Boards and other matters which show that in the year of 1940 in the City of Houston, under the general jurisdiction and sponsorship of the then Governor O'Daniel, a scheme was concocted and apparently it has been partially carried out, to limit and restrict the program of some of our institutions of higher learning in Texas.

Mr. Bobbitt then went on to corroborate Major Parten's testimony concerning the scheme to get control of all the educational Boards in Texas by appointing men who had a definite economic and social philosophy. He specifically referred to "the Houston gag conference" in these words:

> Upon my own responsibility as a citizen of Texas I submit to this Committee that I have heard from honorable and reliable sources of a particular meeting in the city of Houston attended by O'Daniel and a number of his supporters in which this proposition of limiting the academic freedom of some of our institutions of higher learning and of restricting the teaching of certain subjects and the getting rid of certain teachers was generally discussed. It is reported that these learned gentleman decided that such activities on their part could not succeed if their plans were submitted to and considered by the State Legislature, and that the safe and effective method would be to secure control of the governing boards of these institutions of higher learning. It is submitted that Governor O'Daniel did a pretty good job in the matter of placing on some of our governing boards men with "reactionary ideas and strong wills" who would be in a position, and who would be interested in carrying out such a program.

Mr. J. Frank Dobie's testimony before the committee was also highly critical of the political and economic influences being exerted on the university:

> I think the Regents of The University of Texas have tried to build a Maginot line around this institution to keep ideas out. I think in the end it will be [as] ineffectual as the real Maginot line has proved itself. I think that . . . their acts have had the purpose of brow-beating the faculty into a hen house full of old setting hens, [to] have the fear I did, fear free discusison of facts. . . . Coming on down to these three economics professors, instructors, you asked me about them; I've been very much concerned with the motives and with the so-called interlocking of Boards of Regents that's been brought up. If men are all of one kind,

if all of the same bias, if they are one complexion and all compact, they don't have to have conferences to agree on policies; they can pursue the same purposes independently.

I have visited during the last three years several campuses besides my home campus. I would venture that those members of the faculty at the Texas Tech College at Lubbock who voted for Roosevelt in this last election, I venture they voted in a whisper; this purging didn't start right here at The University of Texas. A number of years ago while John W. Carpenter, President of the Texas Power and Light, was a dominating figure on the Board of Regents of Texas Tech, that Board of Regents fired John C. Granberry ostensibly on some, as I recall, some religious point. As a matter of fact, it was for certain economic views he had.

Mr. Karl Hoblitzelle is on the Texas Tech Board now. I understand he received a honorary degree at A & M College not long ago. In his testimony here too, last week, Mr. Strickland said that the concern of the picture show people which he represents, [of] which Mr. Hoblitzelle is the directing spirit in this State, he said the concern of the picture show people is over censorship and he went ahead to tell how pure all the pictures are now that are shown in the theatres controlled by Mr. Hoblitzelle. I think the concern is with censorship. When I left in 1943, *Mission to Moscow* had not yet been shown in the theatres because it was too much in favor of President Roosevelt. I understand that the picture on Woodrow Wilson hasn't been permitted yet in this State on the Inter-State circuit. We are getting that kind of censorship.

There has been a dominating purpose, it seems to me, in the appointment of Regents of various Boards for some time. About 1941 I was talking to my friend, Everett Hailey, who was then in the employ of the J. M. West Estate, J. M. West interests; [I] talked to Hailey about a good Regent for The University of Texas I was very much interested in. I was very much interested in Texas culture at that time, still am, and Hailey was very much interested in it. We talked about Earl Vannel, *Vannel* of Texas, as a potential Regent, and I and Everett said he had spoken to Mr. West about Earl Vannel; Mr. West said he had already recommended to Governor O'Daniel two other Regents, the appointment of two other Regents. I asked who they were and he said, "Dan Harrison and Orville Bullington."

There was one issue in this controversy upon which there was a conflict of testimony and a disagreement upon the facts. This was the telephone conversation between Regent Strickland and Vice-President Burdine, held on Sunday morning October 1, 1944. It is important that this conflict be cleared up, if possible, because it was Dr. Burdine's report of this conversation to me that was the final determining factor in causing me to decide to call the faculty together and bring the whole situation into the open.

Dr. Burdine called me on Sunday morning and said that he had just finished a long 40- to 45-minute, telephone conversation with Regent Strickland. He said that Mr. Strickland had called him. Dr. Burdine reviewed at length the contents of the conversation to me, and we discussed the whole situation at great length. It was our conclusion, then, that the crisis had come, and our conclusion was based largely upon Dr. Burdine's report of what Mr. Strickland had said to him. Dr. Burdine made a full report of this incident to the Senate committee. This is what he said about it:

And then on Sunday morning, October first, Judge Strickland called me . . . about nine . . . and we had a long conversation. The reason I remember that conversation so well, in addition to having repeated it over the telephone to Dr. Rainey, I believe without getting up out of my chair, is that I thought it summarized pretty well the fears and attitudes that had been developing over a long period of time.

Now, I'll just briefly run over the call; I think it was significant, [and] it gave me a terrible jolt. It was just like being hit over the head by a hammer in a way, because I had had considerable hope after talking to members of the Board on Friday, and I thought maybe some progress had been made, but this conversation rather convinced me that the same situation still existed and I frankly thought at that time there was very little hope for improvement. Now, I realize that this conversation was with one Regent only but it's often a question of atmosphere, it's a question of what's gone before over a period of months, and . . . several days later, I made notes of the conversation although I think I remember it just as well now as I did on Sunday when I called Dr. Rainey and told him about it.

He [Strickland] began the conversation by saying that, "Judge Bickett, Mr. Schreiner, and I had been conferring," or words to that effect, I don't know when, I don't know what about, then he began it by asking me, as he told partly in testimony, to get rid of a graduate student who had been discharged from the Army under circumstances which I did not know about. I had learned earlier and had put the boy's name in for investigation. I told him that I had no authority under the rules to discharge a student. That would have to be done through the Dean of Students and disciplinary action, to which he replied the Board would protect me. Well, I rather said in fun, I told him I wanted to know who was going to pay my damages if the boy should sue me for an illegal act if I took such a step. I promised him I would be diligent and had been and would continue to be and on the very next day, on Monday, I called the young man in for a conference.

[Then the Regent] turned to the subject of speech-making by the President. That's not the first time I had heard that but the tone of it was a little bit accentuated. He told me to tell the President that he was making too many speeches which did not concern University business and I believe that was on Sunday and I still believe that he said largely to this effect, "he's running all over the country making speeches to religious groups." . . . He remarked that he supposed the expenses of such trips were not paid by the university. I assured him the expenses were not paid by the university. He said he did not agree with the idea that the President of the university had to make so many speeches and that the President ought to stay in Austin more and attend to university business. When I told him, I remember this so clearly, I told him that I could usually keep the university from falling apart or words to that effect, while the President was away and in reply to that he said to this effect, "well, if that's true there is no need for both of you then." He then pointed out that the limiting of such trips by direct resolution of the Board had been contemplated. That's the thing that scared me. I didn't know how far his authority to make such a statement would go in the matter. And I remember saying, "Oh, Judge, let's don't do that," and that I couldn't imagine anything more insulting to the President than to even think of the Board limiting him in out-of-state trips and speeches.

Now, after we got through with that, we then discussed Communism at the university, another bug-a-boo.

Then, following that conversation, of course, I did call Dr. Rainey because the thing itself hit me rather strongly, the danger. In other words, my morale, considerably. Now, on the following Sunday, which would make it October 8th, a newspaper carried an account or part, that is, [containing] information derived from part of that conversation. I had nothing to do with the publication of that piece in the paper in the sense of having given it to a reporter. I did not. That Sunday afternoon, the day of the publication, the *Fort Worth Star Telegram* got in touch with me rather late that afternoon. They had previously got in touch with Judge Strickland and they told me that in effect he had denied the conversation. Well, they got in touch with me and I told them that I thought I would have to issue some statement on it. I felt as though I would have to protect my own integrity and I presented, I wrote out, I went to the office Sunday afternoon and wrote a statement giving as briefly as I could and as correctly as I could the essence of that conversation.

Now, in my attempt to play everybody fairly and I would take merely the word of the newspaper that there had been a general denial in a way, I decided that since Judge Strickland and I had had rather friendly relations that I would call him and tell him what I was going to do and I think I tried to get him around four in the afternoon but no one answered at his house. I had to give my statement to the *Star Telegram* at about six-thirty that afternoon and about eight o'clock that night I got Judge Strickland. He mentioned in his testimony that [I said] something about apologizing; I didn't apologize. All I did was to tell him . . . something to the effect that I regretted that circumstances were such that the paper thought he had denied that conversation and that I had to clear myself in the matter and so I read my statement to him over the telephone and he told me then that he thought he had made these remarks about speech-making on Friday or something. We have never agreed as to what went into that conversation. But that was a very important conversation to me on account of its nature and its tone and as far as I am concerned that's the end of the talk about that conversation.

In view of the Board's denial of any knowledge of any effort or attempt to limit the President in his speech-making, it is important to point out that Dr. Burdine reported that Regent Strickland began the conversation by saying that he (Strickland) and "Judge Bickett and Mr. Schreiner had been conferring" about matters, etc. It was certainly a fair inference that when Mr. Strickland placed so much emphasis upon the matter of speech-making, he was also expressing the attitude of other members of the Board.

Regent Strickland's version of the conversation was quite contradictory to that of Dr. Burdine. He said in his testimony before the Senate committee:

A. I have stated and I'll tell you about it, I have constructively criticized Dr. Rainey for making out-of-state trips and speeches which Dr. Burdine and I have never discussed; we have never discussed religious speeches. This is the matter that Dr. Burdine and I should have to discuss; probably too much has been said about it. It's one reason why I haven't issued a statement about it until now. I had one written, prepared to file a plea of privilege in some manner at the Houston meeting, but we had a Friday meeting and Saturday, September the 30th, we only transacted business, had an Executive Session, only considered one proposition which Judge Bullington has disclosed to you. We had two men present, two faculty members, which we interviewed at that same meeting. Dr. Burdine told five Regents and Dr. Rainey [that] he was asked about some student that had a general reputation of being an addict of the perverted habit we were discussing and investigating at that time, a student generally discussed and [there were] reports about it. Dr. Burdine said that he had talked to this student, that the student had admitted to him before coming to Texas from another state that he was addicted to that awful habit of perversion that's been described to you, that he came down to the Texas University to reform and he was attempting to reform himself and Dr. Burdine said that since he'd been here they had not been able to discover any of this or [any] overt acts, [and] since he came here under the faculty rules he didn't believe he could be expelled for that reason, that we might have a law suit if they did. He gave this man's name, characteristics, and what he said and he said he had been invited and I assume invited him to leave the University eight or ten times but he said he was hard to handle.

We left about two or three o'clock in the afternoon; three or four Regents went on over to the Commons to eat, [and] had some discussion about it. That's all the discussions I had (that was some time about three or four o'clock in the afternoon) with any Regent. If I mentioned the name of Bickett and Weinert, it was with reference to that thing and only that thing. If you ever believed I ever discussed anything over the telephone about speeches of any character, no other Regent had anything to do with it. I discussed that one subject. We were all pretty well disturbed over this situation, been disturbed for months, and I personally had explained to Dr. Rainey, well not explained, but had complained to Dr. Rainey of the fact that I thought all of us had been complacent. I wasn't criticizing him altogether. We knew they were here waiting to investigate, waiting for the investigation to be complete, some had been identified and I told him in Galveston if nothing was done I would feel like I was condoning a felony. I myself was willing to turn them over to the Travis County Grand Jury. Saturday night this student that Judge Bullington said talked to him in the lobby came and talked to me. I don't want,

I'll disclose his name privately, I don't want him to get in bad; by the way he has said he talked to two men about it.

He disclosed facts to me that I thought were reliable, [and which] convinced me that this man ought to go. The next morning I called Dr. Burdine at his home and told him I had discussed this matter with one or two Regents, that we thought we ought to get rid of this fellow, in any event, whatever it took he ought to get rid of him and that it was up to him and Dr. Rainey to get rid of this man, that they had the authority and power. He [Dr. Burdine] said we might get sued. I said that the Regents would stand behind them; I again reiterated to him [that] if something wasn't done I thought we ought to refer the matter to some proper legal tribunal. And I think I said the Grand Jury. Gentlemen, on my honor, as far as memory can be trusted, that's the only discussion I had with Burdine Sunday morning, October 1st. Dr. Burdine admitted to me later, admitted that conversation but on the end brought in something about making speeches and told me yesterday in the presence of witnesses he had interpreted what I said and meant to infer that I wanted to prohibit Rainey from making religious speeches; [he] said he was going to take it to this committee. I didn't take it to mean I was saying anything about religious speeches. He said I talked to him about out-of-state speeches. I don't know what Burdine is going to say. He's been one of my best friends and told me as late as yesterday he didn't get that inference. He didn't give out the statement; Rainey didn't. They don't know who gave out the statement of it, of the much discussed Sunday morning telephone message.

I had to see the Board of Regents, I thought in good conscience, before I could disclose what had happened in Executive Session of the Board. I got the consent of the Board of Regents in Houston to disclose these facts in a public statement or any other way, [because] there's been so much talk. I have never denied I had that telephone conversation. I deny I ever delivered an ultimatum to Dr. Rainey to quit making religious speeches. I deny that I ever did in any way do that.

Q. (Senator Metcalfe) May I ask a question? Did you ever make a statement, either to Dr. Burdine or anyone else, that the Regents were considering passing a motion or rule or regulation . . . to direct Dr. Rainey not to make so many speeches out of the state?

A. No, sir. I didn't make that statement. I never had conferred with any Board member that I was talking about. He and I had a conversation about that. I never made any issue about it and, as I say, it's difficult for [either of us] to resurrect word for word what was said. I didn't have any dealings with any other Regent. If I used that expression, I expressed my own opinion, I'll be glad to tell you that, I want to tell you anything either personal or business or professional you want to ask me.

But Mr. Strickland said that he did make the following statement to Dr. Burdine in another conference on Friday before the Sunday involved:

I said, "If Dr. Rainey wants to get along he ought to quit making talks about the Regents." He [Dr. Burdine] said, "I think some of you have been talking about him." I said, "You may have something there; if we have, we ought to quit." I said I thought the President ought to quit making all the out-of-state speeches that didn't concern the University. That was Friday morning. Dr. Burdine admitted that to me, told me, half-way apologized for giving out the statement on October the 8th. I said, "Dr. Burdine, why would I want to repeat a thing on Sunday morning when we discussed it freely and fairly on Friday?" He had some little doubt about what I had said about it."

It appears that the only real point of difference between Mr. Strickland's and Dr. Burdine's statements is whether the statements in question by Mr. Strickland were made on Friday or on the following Sunday. It is to be noted also that Mr. Strickland took full responsibility for them, and that he stated that no other Regents were involved. But it should also be noted that it was the Sunday morning telephone conversation that really disturbed Dr. Burdine, and it was also Dr. Burdine's definite impression that Mr. Strickland had conferred with other Regents about it, and that they had even gone so far as to consider Board action to limit my speaking. Certainly it was this aspect of the matter that disturbed Dr. Burdine, and was the determining factor in my decision to bring the issues into the open. I had complete confidence in Dr. Burdine's version of the incident and have never doubted it.

For me this was in the nature of the last straw. For more than two years I had been troubled and vexed with the attitudes and actions of the Board. I had listened to so much petty sniping at the faculty, to ridicule of the concepts of academic freedom and tenure, to sneering references to "the teachers' C.I.O. labor union" (the A.A.U.P.), and to continual insinuations and charges of radicalism and Communism, and I had also become aware that I was the object of their attack. I had been told again and again that they were looking for an excuse to remove me, and that they were engaged in building up a case against me. Certainly my experience bore this out. Messrs. Parten, Bobbitt, and Dobie all testified that this was the case, and that the movement had been under way since as early as 1941.

This, therefore, was all a part of the background and the climate that prevailed, and contributed to my decisions. It had become perfectly clear to the Regents and to their supporters that there was no chance that they could run the university and accomplish their purposes in bringing the faculty under their thumbs as long as I was President. I finally concluded that their purposes were so sinister and detrimental to sound education not only for The University of Texas, but for all education in Texas as well, that I simply had no other alternative but to resist their challenge to the freedom of education in Texas. It was perfectly clear that The University of Texas was the only institution in the state that had any semblance of freedom left. Academic freedom had already been shut off at Texas Tech and Texas A & M, and now these forces had moved in to eliminate it from The University of Texas. I reasoned that others before me had had to make sacrifices and fight to establish our system of free schools in the first place, and that now I and my colleagues were called upon to defend and maintain that they had passed on to us.

It should be noted in this connection that the battle for free schools which was waged in the United States more than a century ago is still going on. The social, political and economic forces that opposed the movement for free schools in the early Nineteenth Century are still active, and have never given up in their efforts to control the schools. These groups that have opposed free schools have been clearly identified by the historians of American education.

These groups and their spiritual successors are the ones who are leading the attacks upon free education at the present time.

Throughout the controversy the Board maintained that the issue of academic freedom was not involved—that they were not against academic freedom and had not violated any principles of this freedom. This insistence, however, simply was not proven by the facts.

They did not, they maintained, violate academic freedom in refusing to re-employ the economics instructors who spoke out in public. The refusal was made not because "those young squirts," as Regent Bullington called them, held economic views contrary to those of the Board, but because these instructors were discourteous and did not show proper respect for the feelings of others, and their "disgraceful conduct" went far beyond the bounds of propriety.

The removal of Dos Passos' *U.S.A.* from the reading list did not violate academic freedom, they claimed, because it was a terribly vile and obscene book. Furthermore, the Regents are charged by law to select courses, textbooks, etc.

They did not violate academic freedom in selectively refusing to approve certain social science research projects. They were just saving the state's money. They had no objection to this research if the applicants wanted to do it *on their own expense.*

In refusing to grant funds for a Sacco-Vanzetti study "the Board could not see how the study of literature could be advanced or society benefitted by the expenditure of the taxpayers money on such a study." The Regents could not see that by this statement they set themselves up as an authority on what was good for American literature, and also as judges of what would benefit society.

They argued that they had two good reasons for their refusal to establish a school of social work: (1) because the Legislature had not appropriated money for it (in fact, the Legislature was waiting for the university to establish it before appropriating money for it, and the university could have set it up with funds in its possession), and (2) because a school of social work would be "teaching socialism" and turning out more bureaucrats for the welfare state, and we had too many of these already.

The Regents claimed that they did not oppose the tenure of faculty members; they simply had no power to guarantee permanent tenure. This was in face of the fact that the Attorney General of Texas had ruled that the tenure rule did not guarantee anybody permanent tenure. The claim of no opposition is hard to reconcile with the Regents' desire to be able to "declare an emergency" whenever they felt the desire to remove somebody, and to thus be able to do it without having to be bothered about charges, hearings, or due process.

Through their actions it became clear that the Regents were bent upon making their own definitions of academic freedom, and upon interpreting the law in such a way as to give them power to run the university to serve their own interests. So-called "labor-union" accrediting associations could not alter or abrogate their oath to do what the law required them to do. Furthermore, these associations were of no importance; had not the sheep and goat raisers of Texas thumbed their noses at their national association and set up their own Texas association? The Regents seemed to believe that Texas could run its university and its schools in the same way, and that Texas didn't need anybody's help in these matters. Texas didn't even need to depend upon the other universities of the nation for the training of the faculty. It could train its own faculties and fill them with good Texans (brought up, one presumes, under the Texas educational system and thus imbued with the "proper" economic and political attitudes).

What chance was there to build "a university of the first class" in the face of such attitudes? They *were* invested with plenary powers to run the university. No one questioned that, and the only hope we had was that they could be persuaded to use their power in harmony with, and support of, the generally accepted standards of all first-class universities. Failing this, there was no recourse other than to appeal to the higher authority—the people themselves, who wrote it into their Constitution, their basic law, that the Legislature was charged with the development of a university of the first class.

This appeal was only partially effective. The immediate reaction of the Regents was that they simply could not function in the face of the charges which the President had made against them, and they made a strenuous, although futile, effort to have these charges withdrawn. When they were unable to obtain the withdrawal of the charges, they were compelled to resign, but in doing so, they used their power like Sampson to pull the whole temple down with them.

THE
REACTION
OF
THE
PRESS:
STATEWIDE
AND
NATIONAL

The university controversy was big news in Texas. It was also given wide attention in the press throughout the nation, for it was recognized that what was happening to education at The University of Texas was of national significance.

The press was quick to respond to the issues of the controversy. Texans love a good fight, and this one promised to live up to their expectations. It had built up over a two-year period, and most observers sensed that things were heading for a crisis and a showdown. When it came, the major issues were already fairly well known and understood by many of the leaders in Texas thought. The details were not known by many, but nearly everybody understood the political set-up in Texas, and reasoned from the knowledge of it that policies then being followed by an ultra-political regime would inevitably lead to an open conflict. They knew from past experience that the leaders of the university would not permit the university to become politically hamstrung and that they would resist any and all attempts to reduce it to political domination.

The incident which brought the controversy to the public's attention, and which led the President to challenge the Regents in an open conflict, was of course the telephone conversation between Regent D. F. Strickland and Vice-President Burdine on Sunday morning, October 1, 1944. It was several days before this information reached the press, and when the story was reported in the press, the storm broke.

From this point, we can let the press speak for itself.

From the *San Angelo Standard-Times*, October 10, 1944:

The University and Politics

Under Dr. Homer Rainey, the University of Texas has gone a long way toward achieving an academic reputation to match its magnificent buildings.

That is a matter of concern, and of pride, to all the people of the State. It is disturbing to most of them that another fight between University Regents and the School Administration appears in the making. Dr. Rainey is reported to have been told "that he was making too many speeches, like those before religious groups." The University President confirms that he has been instructed "to confine my work to University business."

It is our impression that anything which builds good will for the south's largest educational institution is good business. We are at a loss to understand why speeches, even to religious groups, would be detrimental to the University. In fact, appearance by the president in widespread communities of the state would seem necessary to establish a closer bond between Texans and the great state institution which they support.

Nothing can so disrupt an educational institution, and so debase it in the eyes of the public, as politics.

From the *Tyler Telegraph*, October 10, 1944:

Once more the University of Texas has become involved in a political storm that threatens its future progress as a leading center of education for the state.

Dr. Homer P. Rainey, since he became president of the University, has attempted to improve its standards and make it the leading educational institution of the state and nation. Rightly his policy has been one of broadmindedness and tolerance. But like all truly great leaders he has met opposition, and from the very men who should render him hearty cooperation.

Then reference was made to the so-called "gag rule," and the *Telegraph* continued: "It is evident that there is much politics beneath the surface of the dispute."

From the *Evening Valley Monitor* (Mission, Texas) October 10, 1944:

The Hatchet Men Are Here Again

Many Texans were not too surprised this week to hear again from Austin that certain regents of the University of Texas have been poking furtive and thinly veiled threats again at President Homer P. Rainey.

This time the threats have been directed against the making of occasional public speeches by the president off the campus and on topics which might be construed as not strictly academic and appropriately dull.

The Regents acused of making these threats have denied making them. Or at least they have tried to leave the impression of making a denial. But both President Rainey and Dr. J. Alton Burdine, University Vice-President, have stated unequivocally that the threats were made, naming names and giving dates, and neither of these educators has a reputation for being careless with the truth.

If, under the administration of President Rainey, the University of Texas were showing signs of deteriorating into a second-rate institution, and if this deterioration could be laid in any small part on President Rainey's doorstep, then some justification might be afforded for the present hostile attitude of certain regents. But such is not the case. The University of Texas has never enjoyed wider academic recognition than under the administration of Dr. Rainey, despite the handicap of a predominantly hostile board of Regents. . . .

From the *Daily Texan*, the student newspaper of The University of Texas, October 10, 1944, is the story written by Horace Busby, Editor:

The report of the ultimatum to Dr. Rainey "to quit making so many speeches" was being fitted in with a story widely circulated on the campus and over the state before the regents meeting here last month to the effect that Dr. Rainey was to be "fired" at either the September, October, or November meeting of the Board.

From the *Beaumont Enterprise*, October 11, 1944:

Free Speech for All

Regardless of any lack of accord that may exist between the president of the state university and the regents, the right of free speech is something too precious in this country to be interfered with, so long as it is not abused.

From the *Vernon Record*, October 11, 1944:

The average citizen, of course, has no way of knowing the merits of the controversy, but it can be said with safety that friction is not conducive to the best interests of the University. Dr. Rainey has given every indication of being a capable administrator, at least so far as the average citizen can judge. He may not be and if that is true he should be dismissed by the regents, but the occurrence of such incidents as have occurred in the past few years not only under Rainey's administration but in previous ones as well, suggests that much of the fault is with the regents.

From the *Waco Times Herald*, October 10, 1944:

It is a dire misfortune for the people of Texas and a menace to the future progress of this state that a visionless, inept and impotent figurehead remains at the commonwealth's post as governor. We refer to Coke Stevenson. Our remarks today are occasioned by the reactionary clique of University of Texas Regents who seemingly have sworn to get President Homer P. Rainey if it's the last thing they do, and the attitude of this reactionary of all time, Stevenson, has taken toward the plot which now threatens to wreck the University, and put academic freedom of this state on the pages of history alongside Georgia.

Likewise the *Austin American* called upon the Governor to take some responsibility and help to straighten out the difficulties at the university, that "he should do more than just sit and hope." The newspaper urged the Governor to make an investigation of the matter and "make public his findings:"

1. Whether the Board of Regents is failing in its job, and, if so, which regents are responsible.
2. Whether one, or several regents are following a course with Dr. Rainey that is hurting the University.
3. Whether any regent has interests inherently at conflict with the building of a University, free of political manipulation.
4. Whether there are regents attempting policies of restriction and repression harmful to the University, and if so, which regents, and whether there is anybody trying to use the University as a springboard to exceed the bounds of responsible public policy as to academic freedom, freedom of speech and conduct.

But the Governor did nothing to help the situation.

The San Antonio Express headlines read, "Rainey Raps Texas Regents; Lists Restrictive Actions; Faculty Gives Approval with Long Ovation."

On October 14, *The Fort Worth Star Telegram* editorialized as follows:

Most Texans will note with dismay the evidences of disagreement between members of the Board of Regents of the University of Texas and President Rainey, a disagreement which seems headed for an open break.

The *Houston Post* took, perhaps, the most hostile view against the President of the university in an editorial of October 14, "Regents on the Pan":

President Homer T. (*sic*) Rainey of the University of Texas says the rift between himself and the board of regents is not irremediable. We sincerely trust that he is right about that, for the mess is seriously clouding the institution's prospects and jeopardizing its welfare.

However, he leaves little room for hope for that much-to-be-desired end, by laying down his own terms for its acheivement.

Doctor Rainey has assumed the extra-ordinary role of an employe (*sic*) calling his employers upon the carpet. He called the roll of most of the nine members with charges of wrongdoing and indicted some previous members, serving from the time he first became president.

It looks as though they're all out of step but Jim.

However, time seemed to modify the *Post's* view, for twenty-two years later, in its Sunday issue of December 11, 1966, the *Houston Post* ran a half-page story by Harold Scarlett, a *Post* reporter, with a headline across the entire page which read: "He Lost His Job but Won His War."

The article stated:

It was a day of bitter mourning, that day in 1944 for many students at the University of Texas. They marched over to the State Capitol and left in the rotunda a crepe-shrouded coffin inscribed, "Academic Freedom." Today, 22 years later, Rainey can say with quiet satisfaction that the mourning for academic freedom was premature.

In *The Temple Telegram* of October 14 appeared this editorial:

The plain statement made yesterday by Dr. Homer P. Rainey, president of the University of Texas, is to be applauded.

It has been obvious for some time that the University's regents have fallen into the trap which so often snares public boards—that of trying to handle themselves technical details of jobs for which they hire trained administrators.

The regents in this instance, too, seem potently to have adopted a restrictive attitude which does endanger the freedom of thought and expression, and the freedom of research and investigation which are the sources of the university's greatness.

At the outset I would like to express the observation that the University of Texas had made under Dr. Rainey its most conspicuous progress.

The University has grown greatly in educational stature. The leadership of Dr. Rainey has been clean, competent and inspiring.

It is unfortunate that he should have been forced into issuing this bill of complaints against regent interference with the routine operation of the University.

But that he was courageous enough to do it, to put the case before the people of Texas, even at the risk of his own job, is most certainly a big point in his favor.

The El Paso Herald Post, on October 14, wrote as follows:

The Herald-Post believes they [the regents] should either discharge Dr. Rainey or resign themselves.

The present Board of Regents is ill-fitted to be the governing body of the University anyhow. On it are too many legislative lobbyists and too many oil men. The University owns a great deal of oil land and for that reason oil operators and oil lawyers should not dominate the board. As to the lobbyists, they never have a place in the public service. The President of the Board, John Bickett of Dallas, is the telephone company's chief

Texas lawyer and lobbyist. Regent D. F. Striskland of Mission, prominent in the latest row, is the lobbyist for the motion picture industry in Texas.

The Dallas Morning News, in an editorial on October 14 on the "University Issue," said in part:

In the immediate issue the facts cannot be known because the controversy arose from a telephone conversation which is in dispute, but, if Regent D. Frank Strickland either formally or informally gave any such instruction to the University president, he exceeded his authority. As a matter of fact, the full board membership, upon official resolution, has no authority to issue such a rule.

Whether the present board has tended to go beyond its proper sphere of authority, the *News* cannot say. On behalf of Dr. Rainey it must be said that he has put his cards on the table. If his contentions are answerable, the board should answer. If he is vulnerable, he has left himself "wide open" by the definiteness with which he has stated his position.

An editorial in the *State Observer* under date of October 16, 1944, spoke of the business connections of the Board of Regents in these words:

To be specific they have connections with thirteen oil companies, seven public utility companies, ten banks, one paper mill, two railroad companies, three hotels, four lumber companies, four law firms, and fifteen other miscellaneous business groups. . . . If our addition is correct we found these seven regents are rather more or less connected with fifty-nine different business groups.

There is incontrovertible evidence that certain members of this Board of Regents have carried on a species of "Bush-Whacking, Guerrilla Warfare" against the President and other leading members of the faculty for many months—and even years.

In an editorial entitled "Academic Freedom" the *Corpus Christi Caller-Times* on October 19, 1944, said in part:

Getting down to brass tacks right here in Texas, one has but to read President Homer Price Rainey's bill of particulars against certain members of his board of regents for interference with the smooth functioning of academic freedom in this state.

If you don't think it took courage of the highest order for this University president to speak his little piece you know little or nothing of the centuries-old struggle for academic freedom, or what "bucking the board" means to a President or faculty-man.

The *Austin American* in an editorial on October 19, 1944, said in part:

Public groups throughout Texas [as well as] the University faculty and student body sense a real crisis in the University of Texas, now that a long list of conflicts, repressive moves and individually motivated acts of university regents have been put out in the open. . . .

The prestige of President Homer P. Rainey as an educator, and his ability as an executive, are not in dispute. The issue is solely whether individual regents are acting against the interests of the University.

The *Wichita Falls Daily Times* on October 20 wrote in part:

> This much seems clear, that the regents have not caught the vision which actuates Dr. Rainey. His conception of the University is that it is to be something more than a diploma mill, that it should assume leadership in the cultural life of Texas and the southwest. There have been mistakes on both sides, but those interested in the University's welfare are convinced that one big difficulty is the failure of the regents to understand the University's new opportunity, and Dr. Rainey's purpose with relation to it. That is why we find the faculty, the student body, many of the ex-students, and several groups less directly connected with the University, taking Dr. Rainey's side. It is an impressive lineup of forces that has developed within the past week or so, and it suggests strongly that the University's president has far more friends than the regents have.

This was the way matters stood until the Board had its two-day meeting in Houston on October 31 and November 1, at which time the President was removed.

In the meantime there was an enormous public pressure put upon Governor Stevenson to intervene in the controversy. He admitted that he was getting more letters than he could read, and that he could not see all the people who were wanting to talk with him about the matter. But he did nothing, at least not publicly. He said upon questioning from the press that he had not talked with a single regent, and so far as is known he made no attempt to talk with anyone on the university side of the controversy. I made it known that I would be glad to talk with the Governor if he should request it, but I did not feel that I should go directly to him. I had also tried to keep the paths of communication and conciliation open between myself and the Regents hoping that a way could be found to adjust our differences. I had proposed a meeting with them at some retreat for a day or two where we could sit down together in a man-to-man relationship and talk things out. However, these overtures were all ignored.

There was a great deal of pressure put upon the Regents to make a public statement—to answer my charges, and to give their side of the case. But nothing of this kind was done. The Regents did not even get together as a body in the meantime. There must have been a lot of individual communication back and forth between them, but there was no formal meeting. They just let matters ride until their meeting in Houston at the end of the month. Even at that meeting the Board gave the public no answer to the charges that had been made against them. They tried for two days with the help of a faculty committee, and also a committee from the Ex-Students' Association, to get me to withdraw my charges. Failing that they declared an "emergency" and removed me from the presidency without giving any charges against me. Regent Bullington reserved the right to file a personal statement for the minutes of the Board giving his reasons for voting to remove me. When this statement was made public some time later it was also endorsed by three other Regents— Strickland, Schreiner and Stark. (That statement is reproduced in full in Chapter 4.)

After my removal it was announced in the press that six members of the Board had resigned or intended to resign. The resignations of three were announced immediately. They were Bickett, Weinert and Harrison. For some reasons which are still unknown the other three who had announced their intentions to resign did not do so. It is not known whether they presented their resignations to the Governor and were persuaded to withdraw them, or whether they never presented them to the Governor at all. We shall have to wait until some of these gentlemen are ready to tell what happened before we shall know just what took place. All of them and the Governor have remained discreetly silent.

Their resignations were called for by many groups including the Council of the Ex-Students' Association, and again a great deal of pressure was exerted upon the Governor to ask for their resignations and to appoint a completely new Board. All of this availed nothing. The Regents and the Governor stood pat.

Quotations from a few editorials during this period will indicate the public's general reaction.

On November 3 the *Dallas Morning News* said in an editorial entitled, "Ousting of Dr. Rainey":

The removal from office of President Homer P. Rainey of the University of Texas and the resignations of several members of the Board of Regents brings to that institution the greatest crisis, except possibly the imbroglio during the Ferguson Administration, since its doors were opened in 1883 in compliance with the constitutional mandate that the state of Texas establish and maintain "a University of the First Class." The responsibility devolves upon Governor Stevenson. . . . The question of whether the

University will be seriously damaged and handicapped over a long period of years depends upon the wisdom of his action.

However, Governor Stevenson did not find it easy to secure qualified appointments for the vacancies on the Board. A generous interpretation of his inability to find qualified new Regents might be that under the present circumstances he could not persuade men of those qualifications to accept the posts. A new story in the *Austin Statesman* of November 13 reported:

> Governor Coke Stevenson Monday said two men to whom he had tendered appointments as Regents of The University of Texas had declined the offices, while at least two others under consideration had been found "unavailable." . . . Governor Stevenson said that he was "starting over again."

In the meantime, articles and editorials supporting my administration and my stand continued to appear.

From the *Richmond* (Va.) *Times-Dispatch*, November 27, 1944, "Uproar at Texas University:"

> When a faculty as large as that of the University of Texas, numbering hundreds, votes unanimously for the re-instatement of the University's president, and when the students, numbering thousands, join in loud demonstrations toward the same end, it can be taken for granted that the dismissed institutional head has much on his side. . . .
>
> President Rainey is a man of force and vision who never would submit to dictation from political stooges on the board of regents. The now deposed University of Texas president denounced some of Senator O'Daniel's pet notions recently in a New York address. He also told the regents that they were interfering with his prerogatives and violating "the principles of academic freedom of thought and teaching."
>
> This is just the sort of courage and forthrightness which one would expect from Homer Rainey, and the showdown with the regents followed. They have won the first round, but they are far from winning the last. . . . It is greatly to be hoped that the hidebound reactionaries who seem dominant in some phases of Texas life today will taste defeat before they are through with *l'affaire* Rainey. Certainly southerners of good will should rally behind the brawny Texas-born University executive, who has been in battles before, and who, doubtless, is unlimbering his heavy artillery for the fight of his career. He represents the forward looking forces of the south, whereas his detractors belong mainly to those elements which have made this region a butt of ridicule for decades.

The Chicago Sun asked: "Can Texas Save Its University?"

> Blind interests of special privilege have won a sordid triumph over academic freedom at the University of Texas. Details of the case . . . establish beyond shadow of doubt that President Rainey's ouster was the culmination of a long and brazen attempt by entrenched interests actuated by animus against the rights of labor and liberalism generally—

interests bent on stifling free discussion concerning unions, public utilities and other fundamentals of the people's business. Three professors of economics were dismissed by the Board of Regents before President Rainey, having fought a brave but losing fight against encroachments by enemies of education, was fired."

The well known syndicated columnist, Thomas L. Stokes, wrote a series of three editorials on The University of Texas controversy:

1. "National Threat Seen in Texas Attack on Academic Freedom."
2. " 'Letter to Editor' Cause for Firing Professors in Texas."
3. "Familiar, Fantastic Pattern of 'Interests' Throttling School."

In this series of articles, these are some of the things he said:

An issue of academic freedom at the University of Texas is beginning to attract national attention. . . .

From a study of the case, it seems that big economic interests in Texas, for which Senator W. Lee O'Daniel is the spokesman nationally, have moved furtively in on the University.

The Texas case is important nationally because it may indicate a line of attack, insidiously carried out in the field of education, that may be taken in the post-war period ahead. [This proved prophetic.]

It is clear that Dr. Rainey was fighting, in the background, entrenched interests which did not want too free discussion of the rights of labor and of protective legislation for labor, of municipal ownership of public utlities, or to permit comprehensive research into the social sciences or contemporary writing and thinking. These interests are powerful enemies and Dr. Rainey's fight has national implications.

The experiences of Dr. Rainey have a familiar ring: a change in the rule of tenure of professors which, he held, may make it difficult to recruit able men for the faculty; one attempt to require every member of the faculty to sign an elaborate questionnaire, which failed; the attempt, which also failed, to fire another member of the faculty because of views he had expressed, and the denial of a number of research projects.

From *The Washington* (D. C.) *Post*, November 27, 1944:

Freedom to Teach

The issue of academic freedom which has arisen over the deposition of Dr. Homer P. Rainey as President of the University of Texas is by no means exclusively of local concern. It is one more symptom of a dangerous tendency, certainly not confined to the South, though it has found its most flagrant expression there, to make teaching conform to the prejudices and narrow purposes of the economically dominant elements in our society. The tendency is a threat not only to the freedom and growth of our educational system, but is a threat to all free institutions which have their roots in education.

Dr. Rainey's ouster has been investigated by the American Association of University Professors. The general secretary of the Association, Dr. Ralph E. Himstead, declared that a majority of the board of regents "regard their relationship to the faculty to be that of private employer to private employees in which trustees are not regarded as debarred by any moral restrictions beyond their own individual sense of expediency from imposing their personal opinions upon the teaching of the institution or even from employing the power of dismissal to gratify their private antipathies and resentments." Such a view of University trusteeship is inevitably destructive of the University. Able scholars will not serve under such conditions. And neither students or the outside world will respect an institution so dominated.

The press did a first-class job of presenting to the public the facts and issues in the controversy, and also did an excellent job in analyzing editorially the basic issues and setting forth their major implications.

From the foregoing statements by the press certain conclusions seem well justified. They are:

1. The issues were not only local, but national; this local issue was a symptom of a national trend or tendency.

2. The basic issue was academic freedom.

3. The trouble arose because a dominant political group—ultra-conservative—was in control and was trying to impose its social and economic viewpoints upon the University, or to restrict it to the group's points of view. Thus, the conflict represented a clash of social forces, of differing points of view; "profound differences" in points of view. In Texas it was the same political group that was rebelling against President Roosevelt on the national scene—"The Texas Regulars."

4. The Regents had been using a "hacking" process for a long time to get rid of the president, but would not attack him openly.

5. Public sentiment, as expressed editorially, was strongly in favor of the president and opposed to the Regents. There was unanimity of opinion that the president was doing a good job with the university, and the gag rule was considered reprehensible.

6. Responsibility could be laid at the door of Governor Stevenson, both for having appointed the type of Regents and for not using his influence to help correct the matter. Enormous pressure was brought upon the Governor to make an investigation and report his findings, and opinion was almost unanimous that all Regents should resign, and allow the Governor to appoint an entirely new Board. The Board as consti-

tuted was ill-fitted, with too many lobbyists and too many oil men; fifty-nine businesses were represented on the Board.

7. The educational profession, locally and nationally, solidly supported the president and sought his re-instatement.

With these conclusions before us, the question naturally arises as to why and how the Regents were able to win. How were they able to maintain their positions in the face of all the facts against them and the pressure that was brought upon them and the Governor?

In 1945, Mr. Bernard De Voto, historian and editor of "The Easy Chair" in *Harper's* magazine, wrote an evaluation of the controversy which appeared in the August and November issues. His analysis was extremely perceptive. He too, saw in it "not an attack old style on academic freedom," but "the first of a new model."

A digest of his article serves as an adequate summary and evaluation of the issues involved and their significance for higher education in the United States.

What kind of a suppression is this one?

Is it the kind with which we are all too familiar up north—an isolated, sporadic attempt to get rid of one particular thorn in the side of someone, or do the tactics used against Dr. Rainey and more particularly the character of the opposition to him indicate that this may be suppression of a more sinister kind; is The University of Texas, that is, belatedly making the routine fight which most universities have had to make in order to get academic decencies established there?

Or is the episode a sign of the times that foreshadows an attack likely to be made on many educational institutions as the United States rounds into the postwar era? [Emphasis added.]

None of us knows how much of the trouble may be due solely to gang friction in Texas politics—though if such full blown roses of Texas politics as come to national attention are concerned at all, probably we do not need to know more than that. But at any distance anyone can recognize a state of mind, and we may begin there.

[Factors in this state of mind:]

1. Regents said that no particular harm would be done if the A.A.U.P. should blacklist the University, but that unfavorable action by the southern association would be serious.
2. "Powerful forces" working from outside the state were responsible for the whole affair—those vicious organizations turned out to be the A.A.U.P. and the American Civil Liberties Union.
   [Compare O'Daniel's charge that I had been sent to Texas by these "outside forces" to do a job in Texas.]
3. Asked if he believed that a Professor should never question any law, a regent answered: "I don't think anyone has a right to question or violate the law." He told Frank Dobie that: "We should be non-political in our views, which of course precludes any faculty criticism of the Board of Regents."

Another Regent said that: "if he [an instructor in economics] did not think the sit-down strike the most damnable thing in American life, he didn't deserve a place on the University's faculty."

Another believed that all faculty members should be subjected to a "patriotism test."

Another held that *U.S.A.* by John Dos Passos was "the dirtiest, most obscene, most perverted book ever written in the English language."

Strickland told the President that "he was just an employee of the Board. [He] had no right to question a regent's desire to do anything, and should follow the regents' leadership." This was the same regent who would impose the gag-rule on the President and limit his speech-making.

Already a state of mind has been defined—when such men attack academic freedom, no weapon is too vicious, too dishonorable, too dishonest. They *inevitably invoke mass prejudice* and mass fear, and they invariably find that the college involved is a hot bed of homo-sexuality and communism.

So of course our professional lobbyist found that homo-sexuality was "a cancer—growing at the vitals of the University" and he and his gang found communism everywhere.

Such terms are sheer mob incitation, and this particular gang, being in the South, had others available just as useful. Dr. Rainey had been working to widen the educational opportunities to Negroes; he belonged to an organization which tried to bring about better race relations, he was trying to improve negro colleges, he had said in public that there were problems which had to be faced. So his enemies were able to raise the banner of white supremacy and invoke against him the deepest terror in the south. . . . only in the south could the use in an English course of Dos Passos' novel be made a weapon of terrorism. That one is worth lingering on. From any point of view *U.S.A.* is one of the most revealing and most significant novels of our time, and from any point of view it is a work of art and a moral book; but this gang tossed it into every public discussion, finding it a club capable of beating down not only Dr. Rainey but all intellectual inquiry.

The allegation of obscenity was a powerful weapon in itself, but it was a preliminary one; there are other quotations, revealing ones. These are taken from the book's well known reflections on the economic and social system: socialism and communism are mentioned; it is suggested that justice may sometimes have economic roots; Russia is praised; and the sufferings of the exploited are alluded to. *And here is the real offense.* The regents were trying to shock the citizenry with profanity and sex, but what they were afraid of was education in the facts of modern life. What they were afraid of was education.

Thus the regents fired three young economics instructors—another member of the faculty who could not be fired because of the tenure rule had been trying to lead his students to find "ways of making democracy work in the then unusual time of progress of the New Deal." Another had discussed: "the reduction of inequality of income," such as progressive income and inheritance taxes, profits taxes, social security taxes and the like. It was recalled that Dr. Rainey himself, besides being a "nigger-lover" in that he "had been associated with negro-white groups," had come to Texas under suspicion to begin with. The president of a powerful life insurance company had warned the regents that he was "a little liberal."

In a word, Dr. Rainey was administering a University; he was maintaining the freedom of discussion and inquiry which alone makes a University possible; he was permitting the students of the Unversity to be educated. That was exactly what the regents would not stand for and so they fired him. And, determined to root out the evil forever, they broke down the system of academic tenure. Henceforth, the regents would subject every faculty member to scrutiny of his ideas and behavior, and would fire him when they did not like either. Henceforth a prof. at the University of Texas would teach only what the regents told him he could teach. Henceforth, a student there would hear about only such ideas, theories and principles as the regents might think safe, taught in such ways as the regents might think proper.

A group of unscrupulous, but very clear minded men, then, have destroyed the University of Texas as an educational institution—destroyed it, at least, for so long as they or anyone who represents their point of view remain in control. Mr. Frank Dobie does not scruple to call them native fascists. He is using the word carefully: they have faithfully repeated the Nazi attack on the central mechanism of democracy. The service of the regents is to entrenched wealth, privilege, powerful corporations; they are agents of ruthless industry and finance. But clearly they could neither have won nor maintained their victory if they had not succeeded in getting the support of many Texans who want no truck with fascism, and are not enlisted on the side of privilege.

Many thousands of profoundly troubled Texans honestly believe that the regents have been defending their State from outside domination, that they have struck a triumphant blow for individual freedom, that they have saved Texas from terrible evils—that in a way the Republic of Texas has been renewed.

To an outsider it is clear that instead they are regressive and anachronistic, that they have only reared a wall against modern government, modern thinking, modern literature—in short against the modern world. But there lingers in Texas the ghostly memory of an unindustrialized society of a frontier where lack of economic and political safeguards actually worked against the lines. Of pioneer simplicities where frugality and enterprise and minding your own business were enough in themselves to make life excellent. To that golden nostalgia the wall against the modern world seems a defense against all that has proved grievous in the experience of our generation and a promise that Sam Houston will come again.

That is a powerful sentiment, and one easily polarized by a rabble-rouser or an honest deluded man. The Communists were responsible for the New Deal and they intend to inflict a labor dictatorship upon us. They want to debauch your daughters with free love and marry them to negroes. They want to destroy private enterprise and white supremacy. They want to destroy initiative and profit, business and freedom, the individual and the United States. And for this the evil things they teach our children at the University of Texas are responsible. Get rid of Communist professors—who are all homosexuals and New Dealers anyway—and everything will be all right once more. [An eve of great tranquility will come—Woodward.]

We will be back in the days before there was a Depression, before the

New Deal conspiracy was hatched, before labor unions had to be dealt with, before the sacred rights of corporations were invaded, before socialists and bureaucrats in Washington could tell us Texans what we had to do and whom we had to hire and how much we had to pay him, before the foundations of our society were undermined by Atheism and Bolshevism—before Texas became the greatest producer of cotton in the United States, before there were oil wells there, before the most rabid industrialization any American state has seen got under way. Before the modern era began. "Here is a naked form of an old terror; thinking is dangerous." Here are subversive, clear-minded men winning the support of honest, troubled men to another panic-stricken attack on education in the belief that education, which might be the interpreter and enlightened guide of change, is the begetter of change. In more hopeful times we used to believe that such an effort could never succeed—that truth must eventually win, that education could not finally be controlled, that freedom of thought and inquiry were in the end irresistible. We were wrong as hell itself. We have seen the forces of suppression win time after time, destroy a dozen nations, and come within an inch of destroying the world. They can still destroy it—and now we hase seen them win here at home, in Texas. Education is no longer education in Texas. The University of Texas can no longer follow the truth, discover the truth, or teach the truth. It has been taken over by a dictatorship.

So the attack on it was not an attack old style on academic freedom: *it is the first of a new model.* As the waves of reaction gather strength in the years immediately ahead of the United States this same attack will be made repeatedly, in many colleges, always by the same kind of men representing the same interests and forces, employing the same or equivalent means. What has happened at the University of Texas has happened to us all. A Texan, in acute fear of democracy, making an assault on the academic freedom that is one of its implements, assaults everyone who does not fear democracy. That Texan has not only attacked the University of Texas, he has put Yale and Stanford in peril too—and there may be many others dressed in shirts of the same color to take up where he leaves off. [Note: University of Washington, California, Ohio State and others.] The academic community is one, the world of inquiry and appraisal, of the search for truth, and progress, is one. When Texas has lost its freedom we have lost ours.

Dr. Rainey has been fighting our war. So have the thousands of Texans who have been roused to support him. It is an excellent thing that this struggle has not been passed off in Texas as a trivial squabble among pedagogues, but that the state has been deeply shocked and has come to see what is at stake. They have sounded an alert to the Republic, notifying the rest of us that we must be on guard.

In conclusion De Voto stated: (November *Harper's*, 1945)

The actions of the regents, their power and their reckless and contemptuous use of it, the state of mind which they represent, their unmistakable purposes—all these make the affair at the University of Texas a far worse stench in the nostrils of honest men than my brief article was able to describe. . . .

I gather that the [soldiers] of whom Texas is rightly so proud know also that what they have been fighting against is exactly the same sort of philosophy that has temporarily come to dominate their University.

THE
NEW
REGIME—
A
TRAGIC
ERA

After my eviction and the resignation of three of the Board members,
the Board had to be reorganized.
Governor Stevenson appointed three
new members, but in filling these three
vacancies and those that occurred
later, the situation was not improved.
The new appointees belonged to the
same group as those of the old Board,
and it was perfectly clear that the
Governor intended to keep the control
of the university in the hands of those
who had already been discredited.

Mr. Dudley Woodward, a Dallas
attorney, became the new Chairman of
the Board and immediately undertook
to defend the actions of the old Board
and to discredit the deposed President. He tried to offer a defense for
the discredited Regents that they had
not been able to do for themselves.
He did this at a meeting of the Board
in January 1945 even before he and
his fellow appointees had been confirmed by the Senate. He made a four-
hour statement for his reasons for not
"electing" Homer P. Rainey as President of the university. At this meeting

the Board had before it hundreds of petitions—from the faculty, from more than eighty other organized groups, and from individuals—for the President's re-instatement. However, the new Chairman saw it as his function to see that the President was not re-instated, and he had to lay a predicate for this refusal to grant these petitions. His statement was a remarkable document; it was a classic attempt to cloud the issues and further confuse the general public, and to hold the line for his political group.

Although it is interesting to examine Woodward's arguments as they are contained in that statement (which he circulated widely among colleges and universities in January, 1945), it does not seem necessary to reproduce the entire statement, since a greater part of it was a re-hashing of the Regents' arguments in the Senate hearing. Woodward disposed of eight of my sixteen charges against the Board simply by saying that the incidents referred to occurred one to four years in the past. His other main argument was the same as the one used by the Regents, namely that they, not the president, are empowered by the law to run the university. His claiming that he was speaking for the university was ironic, since he had not yet been confirmed as a Regent by the Senate.

However, Mr. Woodward introduced two charges against me that had not been used by the other Regents. The first of these was an insinuation that my administration of Bucknell University (1931-1935) was marred by controversy and was not a successful one. The second charge was an attempt to make it appear that I had made a change in a legislative bill setting up the Dental College in Houston between the time it had been approved by the Regents and its appearance in the Senate. Both of these charges were a complete distortion of fact and of course made me extremely angry. I rebutted Mr. Woodward's entire position, but these two new charges in particular, in a letter which I wrote to him shortly after the publication and distribution of his statement, or his reasons, for his vote against electing me President of the university. This letter dealt in detail with his charges, and the most pertinent parts of it are reproduced here.

You have assumed in your statement "to speak for The University of Texas." Your reason for assuming to do this was that you had "heard little or no discussion of the place of the University in this unfortunate controversy." Such presumption on your part is unwarranted.

I should like to ask you who is "The University of Texas," and what are your credentials for presuming to speak for it? Is the Board of Regents The University of Texas? The answer is certainly "no." The Regents are simply trustees of the people of Texas. Is the faculty The University of Texas? In a very real and vital sense it is. Is the student body The University of Texas? The answer is "yes" to a very considerable extent. Are the Ex-Students The University of Texas? They are surely an important part of it.

Do you speak for any of these groups? You certainly have not represented the student body in your action, for they have been virtually unanimous in condemning the acts of the Regents and in requesting my re-instatement. Surely you do not speak for the vast majority of the faculty, for they voted 92% on a roll-call vote for my re-instatement. You could not have been speaking for the Ex-Students, for their official council voted 2 to 1 in condemning the Regents and in requesting my re-instatement. And can you say that you speak for the citizens of Texas? You have in the Regents' files between 80 and 100 petitions from almost every type of organized group of citizens in Texas expressing confidence in me and asking for my re-instatement. *For whom, then, do you speak?*

You said in your statement, "I wish now to state my reasons for my vote, and *the part I have had in bringing this matter up for attention today*" (emphasis added). You said further that "It should be unnecessary to state *that there must have been compelling reasons to justify bringing the matter up for decision at this time,* especially in view of the position which I took with reference to a somewhat similar suggestion in a letter which I wrote on the 26th of last December, a copy of which went to each member of the Board" (emphasis added). By your own admission there were "compelling reasons" for your decision [not to re-instate me], but what were they? I have searched your statement in vain for them.

You do, however, give us a hint of the reasons when you say: "To that suggestion [electing a permanent president], in my letter of December 26th, I replied in effect that such a course was to me unthinkable for the reason that no man [who] is qualified to act as President of the University would accept appointment from a Board, two-thirds of which might be penalized the following day by rejection by the Senate for having cast a ballot in his favor, and that no man at all qualified to act as a Regent of the University would accept appointment under conditions which might fairly be construed as having influenced his confirmation by a vote on the permanent presidency of the University." May I ask, if it was not just as likely that your vote against my re-instatement would affect your confirmation as would a vote on the permanent presidency? You say that you were at first "in doubt" on that point, but "as I thought through the question, all doubt on that score was relieved." Why was it any more "the exercise of sound democracy" that you express your attitude on my re-instatement than to select a permanent president? In either case the purpose of the action according to your theory of democracy would be to give the people's representatives an opportunity to know in advance what your views were. It would have been equally as embarrassing to me as to any other man to have been elected by a Board two-thirds of whom might have been rejected the next day by the Senate; and it surely would have been sorely embarrassing to you to have rejected numerous petitions for my re-instatement and subsequently failed of confirmation by the Senate.

The conclusion of this reasoning seems to be that you felt sufficiently assured that your action would meet with approval by the Senate. There seems good reason to believe, therefore, that your action was taken because of the [good] effect it would have upon your confirmation. In other words, it was a political maneuver, and you and your political colleagues have dragged the University into politics to serve your own political purposes. This procedure does not square well with your solemn declaration that, 'It, the University, as an institution, is not a party to this regrettable controversy. I am not a party to this controversy and I do not propose to be a party to it; and so long as I have anything to do with the University, it will not be permitted to become a party to it.'

Your statement also indicates that certain members of the Board were considering and trying to get you to consider the election of a permanent president prior to your confirmation. Could your action, therefore, have been a counter move or a compromise with those who wanted to elect a permanent president? In either case, what can be said for the quality of your leadership? You could not have been sincerely considering my qualifications and the vast number of petitions for my re-instatement. You were evidently playing power politics. An honest statement from you on these points would be helpful in understanding "the part (you) played in bringing the matter up for decision."

The Governor had time and again assured the public that he was selecting Regents who had an open mind on the University situation. He even went so far as to say in a press conference that he would not be opposed to my re-instatement. That was for the Regents to decide. Why then did you feel compelled to show your bias against my re-instatement before your confirmation . . . , especially since you had told at least three personal friends of mine that you were certainly going to have a conference with me before you came to a decision upon the controversy? Would not every rule of justice and fairness dictate that a conference with me, since I was the other principal in the controversy, was necessary if you were going to pass a valid judgment? It looks very much as if you were pressured into the action which you took. Tell us the facts about what happened. Tell us why you apparently changed your plans so suddenly immediately prior to the meeting of the Board on January 26th. If your actions were in the best interests of the University, full knowledge of what you did would be beneficial in helping everyone to arrive at a better understanding of the University's problems.

You made a malicious attack upon my administration at Bucknell University. I am happy to have my record at Bucknell investigated by any honest and sincere person. But in my opinion your motives were neither honest nor sincere. It is indeed singular that your research through "academic" channels should turn up the one former member of the Bucknell Board of Trustees who had opposed some of my policies. There were 30 or more other members of that Board that you might also have consulted if you had been seeking an honest and sincere evaluation of my work there. It is also singular that the man whom you consulted is badly discredited in his own profession, [and] . . . was recently turned down by a vote of his colleagues on the Bucknell Board for a continued place on that Board. This was done in June, 1944. This is the same Board that elected me to membership when I resigned as President of Bucknell to become Director of the American Youth Commission. You labored in your statement to create the impression that my administration at Bucknell was a failure and that I left just ahead of the ax. It isn't customary, is it, for a Board of Trustees who are supposed to be at the point of dismissing a President to honor him by voting him unanimously a place on their own Board? This was done in my case, and I could still be a member of that Board if I had not resigned on my own accord after I came to The University of Texas.

Another regular singular fact connected with the use of your source of information from Bucknell is that at about this same time there appeared a newsletter sent out of the Librarian's Office of the Medical School in Galveston and signed by Miss Mildred Robertson, in which this question was asked: "Wasn't this man also relieved of his similar post at Bucknell University for like insubordination?" This coincidence leads to the presumption that you and one or more members of the Medical School staff were using the same "source" of information. If you are honest and sincere why withhold the 'academic' source of your information? Surely, if the "source" is a reputable one, only good could come from a frank statement of where you got your information.

But the "academic" source of your information is not nearly so reprehensible as the ways in which you used the information. You used it anonymously. You apparently did not even make it known to the other members of your Board. But you gave the name to the representatives of the Southern Association of Colleges who were present upon your invitation and who were at that time making an official investigation of the University. Why the distinction?

This conduct on your part violates every known rule of evidence so carefully worked out by your own profession over hundreds of years in order to guarantee to all men a fair and impartial trial. You surely knew that such evidence would not be permissible in any court in our land. A representative of the Ex-Students' Association, a distinguished member of your profession, was present and publicly protested your procedure, but to no avail.

You made this attack upon me without granting to me beforehand the opportunity of a personal interview or without according me, in line with every common legal decency, the privilege of hearing the "evidence" as you unfolded it, or of defending myself against the distorted facts which you presented in open hearing. I believe that all loyal friends of the University, and all honest men everywhere, will repudiate your pretended fairness and your sophistry.

There is one further point about your use of the Bucknell case that should not be overlooked, and that is, that your use of it condemned the integrity of the Board of Regents who elected me to the Presidency of The University of Texas. The clear implication of your attack is that those members of that Board were careless and negligent in their investigation of my record at Bucknell. Mr. Woodward, your arrogance and presumption are amazing. You presume to set up your investigation of two months and your one discredited "academic" source of information against the judgment of a former Board of Regents, a distinguished Ex-Student Committee, and an outstanding Faculty Committee, all of whom labored diligently for approximately eighteen months in search of a President for the University. Furthermore, you wave aside the opinion of a vast majority of this Faculty who have worked under my administration for more than five years, and the friendship and loyalty of practically the entire student body, to say nothing of the Ex-Students and the general public. Indeed, you must have had "compelling reasons" or else your egotism is colossal.

What was your real reason for omitting an evaluation of my experience as Director of the American Youth Commission? How can you think that that experience had no bearing upon my qualifications to become President of The University of Texas? It was a study of the needs of all youth in the United States, and an effort to provide "a comprehensive program for their care and education." Would not such an experience as that better qualify me to furnish leadership in providing a program of education to meet the needs of Texas youth? The presumption is strong that you omitted it purposely, and that your purpose was to find someone, *just anyone*, who was willing to give you an adverse report upon any part of my past work. This type of conduct on the part of the Chairman of the Board of Regents of The University of Texas cannot possibly inspire confidence in your leadership. Your purpose was to discredit me, and you resorted to unworthy methods in attempting to do it.

Your use of the Dental College incident is equally as reprehensible. You tried to create the impression that the Board of Regents had had its attorney, Mr. Scott Gaines, draft a bill to be submitted to the Legislature, and that after he had done so, I changed the draft of the Bill before presenting it to the Legislature; and that my conduct in this respect was reprehensible and made me unworthy to remain as President of the University. This is a gross distortion of the facts. The Board of Regents never at any time drafted or had their attorney draft a Bill for their approval. All the Board of Regents did was to approve the policy of accepting the Dental School on condition that the Legislature would approve their acceptance of it and provide the appropriations necessary for its support. The matter of drafting the Bill and getting Legislative approval for it was left entirely in *my* hands. It was I, and not the Regents, who invited the University's attorney to assist *me* in drafting the Bill. It was my full responsibility as the executive agent of the Board to prepare the Bill and to secure its passage in the Legislature. . . . [The] change which I made in the attorney's draft was simply to write into the Bill the procedure provided in the Regents' published Rules and Regulations for the nomination of all faculty personnel—namely, that all members of the faculty shall be appointed by the Board of Regents upon the nomination of the Dean and the President. This is simply the procedure followed not only by the Regents of The University of Texas, but by all universities with which I am acquainted. That is all there was to the Dental College matter. It did not in any way change the relationship between the President and the Board of Regents, as you say it did. Evidently you are not familiar with the Regents' published Rules. Your insinuations are malicious and inexcusable. Not a single member of the Board of Regents ever raised any question with me about the Bill for the Dental School.

What possible objection could be found to writing the Regents' own Rules of Procedure into the Law setting up the Dental College? If you were sincere and honest in seeking all the facts of the case, why did you not consult me about it? You state that, "in view of the character of this transaction, I have been at unusual pains to discover the exact manner in which it occurred. . . ." The fact that you did not consult me about it is *prima facie* evidence that your statement is untrue. Would any honest and sincere person in search of the truth about any important matter form a judgment without hearing evidence from both parties to an issue? Here again, you have violated not only the elementary ethics of your profession, but the common courtesy that any gentleman will always accord another.

The Bucknell case and that of the Dental College were the only new data injected into the controversy in your statement. For that reason I have dwelt upon them at some length, in order that the public may get the true picture in each case. Your distorted use of them carries this controversy to even a lower level than another Regent's use of the homosexual case.

One of the most interesting aspects of your four-hour harangue was your attempt to defend the old Board and to evaluate the charges I had made against this Board in my report to the General Faculty on October 12, 1944. In view of the fact that the old Board never refuted these charges, I am sure that it must have taken a great deal of outside pressure for you to have assumed the role of the Great Apologist for them. Further, in attempting to explain away these charges by pointing out that the events or incidents upon which the charges were based occurred five or three or two years prior to the issuance of my report, you, as a learned lawyer, apparently departed from your legal training in minimizing the value of precedents. You dismissed at least eight of my sixteen points with no more answer than that they occurred a number of months in the past. Certainly, I deliberately chose a series of incidents covering quite a period of time for the purpose of showing a continuous violation of academic freedom and good principles of University administration. In endorsing and apologizing for the actions and policies of the old Board and its individual members, you have not contributed very much to an "era of tranquility" in the affairs of the University nor have you gained that confidence in your leadership which you apparently so much desire. Your attempt to answer in behalf of the old Board my sixteen points leads me to raise with you a question to which the faculty and all friends of education are entitled to have from you a forthright answer: do you endorse and subscribe to the policies and practices of the old Board of Regents, three members of which are on your Board? Apparently you do.

Your attitudes and the principles of University administration set forth in your statement of January 26h lead me to make the following observation: if you, as a member of the Board of Regents, should rob the University of any or all of its permanent endowment, the laws of the State would require that you be committed to prison; but I affirm that your conduct as represented by your immediate past actions is robbing the University of a far more precious value than its permanent endowment. You, as the Chairman and leader of its official Board, are sacrificing its honor and its integrity. Without these virtues it cannot hold its place among the great universities of the nation.

There was one other episode in my relations with Regent Woodward which should be mentioned here.

When I was elected President of the University I was also given a professorship in the School of Education. It is a rather general practice to give administrators a professorship; it is designed to provide them with tenure, since as administrators they have no tenure and serve "at the will of the Board."

I was careful to discuss this arrangement with the Dean of the School of Education, Dr. Pittenger, before I accepted the presidency of the university to make sure that he would approve a professorship for me in his school. He agreed to this very cordially, and assured me of his full cooperation. He and I were already well known to each other, since we were both deeply interested in the field of public school finance. Each of us had written a book in this area. In addition, I had taught for him in two previous summer sessions at The University of Texas.

When the Regents removed me from the presidency of the university on November 1, 1944, nothing was said about my professorship. Was I to assume that I could move over to the School of Education and resume my teaching? To do this would require some definite action on the part of the Regents and the Dean of the School of Education. But, since the Board of Regents was not re-organized until the following January, there was a period in which my status as a professor was in doubt. This confusion, however, was removed as soon as Mr. Woodward and the new Board of Regents took over the administration. Mr. Woodward's position was quite clear. He reasoned that since I had done no teaching since becoming President, my professorship was a nominal and *pro forma* arrangement and had no real meaning. He said that he saw no reason to change my status as a professor so far as he was concerned. I could remain this kind of professor—with no assigned duties and, of course, no salary. Since I was not financially independent I could hardly afford to accept this arrangement.

Mr. Woodward, much to my surprise, was abetted by Dean Pittenger of the School of Education. As I stated above, Dean Pittenger had, at the time of my appointment, given his hearty approval to a professorship for me, but when the matter became a possible reality he demurred and would not recommend an active professorship for me. My disillusionment at Dean Pittenger's lack of personal courage in this case was a matter of great regret to me—not that I wanted the professorship or would have accepted it if offered; my disappointment was in Dean Pittenger's weakness.

Regent Woodward tried very hard to convince the faculty, the educational profession and the public that he was a champion of academic freedom, and that under his administration there would be nothing but the strictest adherence to sound principles of university administration. In fact, he promised a great period of tranquility in the university:

> An era of tranquility has begun in the administration of The University of Texas. Dr. Painter, serving as acting President at the request of the Boards, enjoys, as his successor must enjoy, the full confidence and respect of the Board and of its individual members. The Board values and depends upon him as its expert adviser because of his fairness, wisdom and experience; it holds him forth to the world as its responsible agent because of his integrity and dependability. . . .

This promise of an era of tranquility for the university was received by the faculty with a quite sizeable grain of salt, and by Bronx cheers in some quarters. It also inspired one of the choicest bits of literature that has ever come out of a controversy of this sort, worthy of republication here. Unfortunately, its authorship is unknown.

Thus Mammon spake

. . . All things invited
To peaceful counsels, and the settled state
Of order, how in safety best we may
Compose our present evils, with regard
Of what and where we are, dismissing quite
All thoughts of war. Ye have what I advise.

Milton, Paradise Lost, Book II

An era of tranquility has begun in the administration
of the University.

D. K. Woodward, Chairman of the
Board of Regents, University
of Texas

TRANQUILITY, A POEM

Tranquility, thou languid Goddess, rise!
Stretch thy rheumatic limbs, and rub thine eyes;
Thy worshippers attend, a gaping throng,
To hum thy glories in obedient song.
All bow to thee in this, illustrious one;
Under thy aegis Nothing Shall Be Done.
No faithful slave of thine, who hopes to live,
Shall e'er Accentuate the Positive;
No restless intellect shall dare to chafe
Against thy solemn precept, "Be Ye Safe."
With blazon'd mottoes now thine altars glow:

Free Enterprise! God Save the Status Quo!
Down with That Man! and Don't Forget the Alamo!
See Pictor, Priest and Champion of thy name,
Kindle before thy shrine a smoky flame.
Say why he left an ancient, honored trade
To Sport with Woodward in the chequer'd shade;
To wanton with th' elusive millionaire,
Or with the tangles of sweet Strickland's hair;
Whence this desire for better things in life:
A Just ambition, or a climbing wife?
Behold him now, no more the threadbare scholar,
Valiantly working for the Regent's Dollar.
He lisps and mutters, Goddess, in thy praise,
But no one understands a word he says.
Lo, how he dances to the piping tune
Of Barker, Battle, Patterson, Calhoun!
See next approaching an egregious band,
Three clumsy wielders of the iron hand,
Bullington, Strickland, Schreiner—one in three—
A latter-day unholy trinity.
Benevolent, victorious, benign,
Rich gifts they bring to deck the Goddess' shrine;
Two mortgages, foreclosed down Kerrville way,
Three copies (freshly marked) of *U.S.A.*,
Four dummy profs to set up as decoys,
Five dinners, seven moving-picture passes—
Prizes for all who want to kiss their a—!
Well-pleased, the Goddess eyes the goodly store,
And greets the fitting tribute with a snore.
Now Woodward comes, and ushers in a train
Of handmaids for the Goddess' new domain:
Malice and Slander glare with baleful eyes,
Followed by swarms of Legalistic Lies;
And o'er them all flits that two-headed fairy,
Suggestio-falsi-et-suppressio-veri.
Proud of his cohorts, Woodward hails the Queen,
And smiles with slitlike mouth upon the scene;
"While we have power," he cries, "to fight for thee,
Justice shall ne'er disturb Tranquility!"

Behold three ancient worshippers appear,
And greet bold Woodward with a quavering cheer.
First Battle, reverend sirs, comes footing slow;
He fought, 'tis said, for Freedom long ago,
But fallen now, alas! to propagate
Reactionary views and real estate.
Calhoun is next, specious in argument
(A fellow-servant at the shrine of Rent):
His innuendoes o'er the crowd he strews
And kicks about him with a dead man's shoes.
Malignant, impotent, see Barker stand,
A wooden broadsword in his palsied hand;

He thrusts it forth with ineffective blows,
Intent to terrify the Goddess' foes.
His threats they scorn; his spite they deprecate.
The menaces of eminence have weight,
But who will tremble when the foe is second-rate?
A crowd not large but dense, a motley throng,
See now press forward, two and twenty strong.
Here Belial Fitzgerald whines and sobs,
Patterson plans new legislative jobs,
Weak Manuel stutters his despairing note;
Moore, apoplectic, seeks a record vote.
Such are thy servants, O Tranquility,
Such were, and are, and evermore shall be.
Receive them kindly, for they love thee well;
Against their power let no rash soul rebel.
Keep thou our Alma Mater safe in pawn,
Till life and mind are lost in one vast tranquil yawn.

The prophetic insights of the author of "Tranquility" were remarkable indeed. Regent Woodward talked "Peace! Peace!" but there was no peace. The conflict could not be buried and forgotten; its issues were too far-reaching to be smothered.

There were present at the Regents' meeting, at which Chairman Woodward presented his four-hour defense of the former Regents, representatives from Phi Beta Kappa, the American Association of Universities, the Southern Association of Colleges and Secondary Schools, and the American Association of University Professors. Mr. Woodward said in their presence: "The University needs, and I think it still has, and it will certainly try to keep and improve its preferred standing with all of these groups."

Evidently, these groups were not favorably impressed with Regent Woodward's presentation, for Phi Beta Kappa, the Southern Assocation, and the A.A.U.P. all took adverse action against the university subsequently. The Southern Association made an investigation and placed The University of Texas on probation on July 22, 1945. Phi Beta Kappa also made a careful investigation and condemned the actions of the Regents.

The A.A.U.P. made the most careful and thorough investigation of all the groups, and after more than a year of consideration issued its report in June 1946, at which time The University of Texas was placed upon its list of censured colleges and universities; the university remained upon that list for *nine years.* This is a clear indication that the A.A.U.P. was not, for nine years, convinced that proper standards and conditions had been restored in the administration of the university.

When the Southern Association released its report in July 1945, placing the university on probation, Chairman Woodward was greatly embarrassed, and released a public statement under date of August 5, 1945. In this statement he said a number of things:

> The reflection thus cast by the Association upon the standing and reputation of The University of Texas is serious and far-reaching. It requires the issuance of this statement by me in my capacity as Chairman of the present Board of Regents in order that the position of the University, as distinguished from that of certain of its former officers and Regents, may be clearly understood. . . .
>
> No word in the Report gives effect to any act of the present Board of Regents, or any other representative of the University after November 1, 1944. Probation was imposed upon The University of Texas on July 22, 1945. It was justified, if at all, by *all* of the facts which had occurred up to that date. . . .
>
> The action of the association in convicting the University without considering the facts which occurred after November 1, 1944 was unjust and will be denied approval by fair-minded people.

He then listed a number of things that the new Board had done to correct the difficulties caused by its predecessors. Nevertheless, The University of Texas remained on probation by the Southern Association for one year.

What happened under Chairman Woodward's regime is an essential part of this study. We should, therefore, take a close look at some of the significant facts of his regime. In effect, Woodward became the President of the university. Dr. Painter was a figurehead, a front for Woodward. The faculty never accepted Dr. Painter as President; it had no confidence in him nor respect for him. Woodward became the spokesman for the Board and for the university, and he tried to whip the Board and everybody into line. He formulated the policies of the university and the Board and even "lectured" the Legislature. He became the "white-haired oracle" of the plutocracy in Texas. He and his group had gotten rid of the radical President, and all was well on the forty acres under his benevolent and guiding hand.

But what about all those radical professors? Were they not still there? Yes, but their influence would be harmless.

They would now become good boys, and his influence would assure the university's adherence to "true economics" and sound values. The people were to trust him and have no worries. He would tell President Painter what to do, and no one else with the experience of President Rainey's fate in mind would dare challenge the power and authority of the Board. He knew what was good and right for the university. His motives were high and pure. The unfortunate Rainey episode would soon be forgotten, and the university could return to its rightful place in the life of the state.

The power of the Regents had been shown to be supreme. It had been established that the Presidents in the future would surely understand the time-honored and divinely sanctioned principles of "principal and agent" and no President would violate this principle in the future. Presumably all would meekly do what they were told to do.

When it became clear that Woodward could not make the faculty swallow a puppet president, it was necessary to make a new approach to the administrative problem. The Regents plumped for a chancellorship. They would seal off the President and appoint a super-President, thinking this would add great dignity to the administration and give them an opportunity for a new start. But best of all, Woodward saw in this an opportunity for himself personally to consummate his ambitions, and to dignify his de facto powers in a highly respectable academic position.

The story of the development of the chancellorship idea, and the selection of the first chancellor, is an interesting one.

Regent Woodward's regime as Chairman of the Board of Regents came to an end in November 1952 by the presentation of his resignation as Chairman of the Board. His statement to the press announcing his resignation was an ironic one. He bemoaned the fact that *his* program for the university had not been successful in the Legislature, and laid the blame for its failure upon the Texas Manufacturers' Association. This was both a revealing and an ironic confession for him to make. It sounded like *certain economic forces* in Texas were interested in blocking the program of the university. This was a remarkable bit of news coming from a Regent. It would have been regarded as a "radical" or "subversive" statement if it had come from the President, or any other officer of the university. Its irony lies in the fact that the very same group that fought me, and whom Mr. Woodward tried to represent and serve, had now repudiated him and cast him aside. He was no longer useful to them, and they were ready for some new leadership. At the time of his resignation it was already asserted by the press that he could not be re-elected Chairman of the Board at the forthcoming reorganization meeting in January 1953. A close friend of Governor Shivers was slated for his part. Woodward had lost his magic touch and had failed ot make himself chancellor. President Painter had neutralized him on this move. Woodward had, however, selected a chancellor of his own choosing, expecting, of course, that he would be able to continue to make the policies and run the university as he had been doing since becoming Chairman of the Board. This was a serious miscalculation, for the new chancellor was a man of high character and integrity—one who did his own thinking, and who had made up his mind that as long as he was chancellor he would carry out his duties in harmony with the "generally accepted standards" of a great university. He made it plain on several occasions that he was chancellor in fact as well as in name, and that neither Chairman Woodward nor anyone else could "deliver him."

This fact proved both embarrassing and disappointing to Regent Woodward. Under his theory of principal and agent (Woodward was the principal, of course) it was embarrassing to have an agent who told his principal that the Regents would have to follow his recommendations on matters within the university. Furthermore, such conduct on the part of the chancellor was extra-legal, in that it took from the Regents their powers under the law to operate the university. It was also quite disappointing to have one's appointee show such ingratitude as to think for himself and to put his principal on the spot with his political cronies, and to give aid and comfort to the Manufacturers' Association, which was blocking the principal's program in the Legislature.

It is no wonder that a new principal was called for. The old one had lost his control. He was beginning to let the university be operated according to generally accepted standards. This would never do. It would lose the political groups all the ground they had gained in the last nine years.

Thus the Woodward regime ended in political defeat and personal rejection. Out with it went President Painter and two Vice-Presidents.

What can be said for this regime? It did not restore faculty morale and it failed to bring tranquility. It did not get the university off the A.A.U.P. censured list. It made no notable additions to the faculty. It did not regain the confidence of the educational profession, nor even of the people of Texas. It had lost, or failed to obtain, the support of the Texas Manufacturers' Association according to Woodward's confession. It had not solved the medical school problem; in fact, it had further confused that problem by allowing the creation of a second medical school in Texas, thus dividing and further dissipating the revenues for medical education. It had allowed a further dissipation of its resources by maintaining a Graduate Medical Center in Houston. This all clearly indicated a lack of a sound policy for medical education in Texas. In fact, the Board of Regents during this time had not had a medical policy; it had simply been following a course of expediency, dictated by the political medical profession in Texas, and by geographical political pressures which are so powerful in centers like Houston and Dallas.

Another major responsibility of the Regents and a promise by Chairman Woodward was not fulfilled—that of the selection of a President. Mr. Woodward, in an announcement of policies adopted unanimously by the Board of Regents, February 16, 1945, said:

Because of Dr. Painter's insistence that his service as President be temporary only, the Board is faced with the difficult duty and responsibility of finding a worthy successor for the high office he fills with such distinction. It approaches this task diligently but without haste and with full confidence in its ability to find a qualified man who will accept the challenge of this matchless opportunity.

There is much to be said about the items included in this statement. In the first place, there is the question of why Dr. Painter was insistent "that his service as President be temporary only"? The answer to this question is to be found in the attitude and actions of the faculty. When Dr. Painter was selected as acting President by the Board that removed the President, the faculty were not at all happy about it, and the question was raised about faculty approval, or an expression of confidence and support from the faculty. The faculty agreed to give Dr. Painter their support on two conditions, namely: (1) that his tenure would be *temporary*, and (2) that he would not accept the permanent presidency if it were offered him. These conditions were expressed in a written agreement between the faculty and Dr. Painter and signed by Dr. Painter.

However, this pledge to the faculty was disregarded and broken by Dr. Painter later when, after all, the Board decided to tender him the permanent presidency. The Board at its meeting on a Friday offered Dr. Painter the presidency. This offer was made without consulting any faculty committee or ex-student committee for their recommendations or approval. The offer was made solely at the discretion of the Board. Although Dr. Painter asked for some time to think it over, he did not consult the faculty nor ask to be released from his pledge. He deliberated less than twenty-four hours before accepting the offer.

The Board had clearly failed to recognize the faculty's interest by its failure to ask the help and advice of the faculty in the selection of a president; this was certainly a violation of just plain good procedure, and a failure to follow the tradition of other previous boards. The additional failure to consult with the Ex-Students' Association on such an important matter as the selection of a President made the whole procedure highly irregular on the Board's part. It is not the way good Boards ordinarily proceed in the significant responsibility of selecting a President. Furthermore, this Board certainly knew of the faculty's attitude toward Dr. Painter, or it easily could have found out. It is notable that the Board made no attempt to consult with the faculty about it. This Board also must surely have known of Dr. Painter's pledge to the faculty regarding the permanent presidency. In that event, why would the Board put Dr. Painter on that spot, and why would it jeopardize its relations with the faculty by naming Dr. Painter President under such circumstances, without even consulting with the faculty about it? This doesn't make sense.

What would he do now in view of his signed pledge to the faculty that he would not accept the permanent presidency? He might well have done something like this: He might have called the faculty together and said: "The Board of Regents has offered me the presidency of the university, but I have a pledge with you that I would not accept it. Since I made that pledge conditions have changed. The Regents seemed to be pleased with my leadership and have expressed their confidence in me by offering me the presidency on a permanent basis. In my experience in the acting-presidency I have come to like the position and feel that I have the qualifications for it. In view of these points I would like to be free to accept the post, and, therefore, I would like to ask you to relieve me of my former pledge to you and further to ask your confidence and support."

This would have been a straightforward, honorable thing to do. It would have preserved his integrity, and it would have recognized the faculty's rightful interest in the matter.

But there is another basic question: Had the Board made a "diligent effort" to find a qualified man to take the presidency? The answer to this question is obviously, "No." In the Board statement of policies released February 16, 1945, it said:

Because of its especial qualifications and interests, the Board calls upon the faculty of the main University to choose from its members a representative committee of convenient size to advise with the Board in its selection of a president. The Board will from time to time, and in such ways as may be found convenient and effective, seek advice from the officers and faculties of the several branches of the University and from qualified persons of cultural background throughout the state, including, but not limited to, former students of the University.

Here is outlined a good procedure for the selection of a President, and a definite promise that this procedure would be followed. What happened to this procedure and this promise in offering the presidency to Dr. Painter? Was a faculty committee ever appointed and was it consulted in reference to Dr. Painter? Was the advice of the ex-students of the University sought? The answer to all these questions is, "No."

Why did the Board act in such an unorthodox manner, and why did it violate its expressed promise to the faculty and ex-students and to the general public? These are important questions, because unless the Board could give satisfactory answers to them, it is *prima facie* evidence that they had defaulted upon their trust, and failed to fulfill a major responsibility of a Board, which is the selection of a President.

If Dr. Painter was really a qualified expert educational

adviser for the Board and worthy of this high position, all of these things were known to him and he would have acted accordingly, and he would have insisted that such good procedure be followed for the sake of his own integrity, and for the sake of his good relations with the faculty which was absolutely essential to the success of his administration. For his part, the least that Dr. Painter could have done, to preserve as many of the values in the situation as possible, would have been for him to take the faculty into his confidence and ask for their advice and support. To have done this would have gone a long way toward encouraging the faculty's respect for him and their confidence in his integrity.

But Dr. Painter didn't do any of this. He accepted the presidency the morning after it was offered, without as much as ever mentioning the matter to the faculty. The faculty were stunned and bitter. Their confidence in both Dr. Painter and the Board went out the window, and it was never restored during the Woodward-Painter regime. What values could come out of an administration launched in such a manner, not only in violation of all good standards of procedure, but in violation of expressed promises by both Dr. Painter and the Board?

There is a very plausible explanation of why the Board of Regents didn't follow its promise to select a qualified man for the presidency, but instead offered it to Dr. Painter It is the fact that no leader in American education would accept the presidency of the university under the conditions which prevailed there at that time. A preliminary investigation on the Board's part would have revealed this fact to them. It is quite likely, therefore, that the only choice the Board had was to offer it to Dr. Painter.

If the Board had followed its announced procedure of February 16, 1945, and had selected an outstanding President and supported him with the policies which it had approved, it would have been the very best thing that could have happened. It would have had many fine results. It would have restored faculty confidence in the educational profession and would, in a very short time, have brought about the removal of censure by the A.A.U.P. It would have brought about confidence generally, and indeed, would have been the surest way to tranquility. This was the way the faculty and ex-student committees had urged upon Governor Stevenson, but it was turned down at that point by the Governor, and he will have to bear his share of the responsibility for the failure to meet the university's need. Instead of acting as it was recommended to him, he did not call for the other Regents' resignations, and when he made his new appointments he appointed Regents who were definitely partisan in their attitudes.

There is only one conclusion that is justified from all these considerations, and that is that it was desired to keep the control of the university in the hands of the political group which had taken over and had caused all the trouble. The maintenance of their control outweighed the necessity of doing a constructive and worthwhile job in behalf of the university. They had set their hands to the plow, and there was no turning back. They had undertaken to do a job, and they were going through with it. The welfare of the university was secondary to the solidifying of their political control over it.

It was during this time that the American Association of University Professors gave their verdict on all these issues in their report of June, 1946. Because of the professional standing of that group, and because of the thorough investigation which they made of all the issues involved, their report was of great value.

The American Association of University Professors was organized in 1915 with the fundamental purpose of protecting the freedom of research and teaching among American scholars and teachers. Over the years it has evolved a set of principles relating to these freedoms that have been accepted and endorsed by practically every major educational profession in the nation, such as: The Association of American Colleges, American Library Association (adapted for librarians), Association of State Colleges and Universities, United Chapters of Phi Beta Kappa, American Catholic Historical Association, and many others. Many individual colleges and universities have adopted these principles and written them into their by-laws for the governing of their respective institutions, including The University of Texas. These principles had been a part of its by-laws for many years.

These principles are relatively broad. They state simply that (a) "a teacher is entitled to feel freedom in research and in the publication of the results;" (b) "the teacher is entitled to freedom in the classroom in discussing his subject;" and (c) "the college or university teacher is a citizen, a member of a learned profession, and an officer of an education institution. When he speaks or writes as a citizen he should be free from institutional censorship or discipline . . . but . . . he should be accurate at all times, should exercise appropriate restraint, should show respect for the opinions of others, but should make every effort to indicate that he is not an institutional spokesman."

It was the numerous violations of these principles by the Board of Regents that constituted the chief complaint of the academic community against them.

It should be noted that this Association has no legal power or control over a given institution. Its strength is dependent entirely upon its *moral* force. Whenever an institution is accused of violating its principles, the Association sends a small committee, usually three in number, of professors selected from institutions across the country to make an "on-site" investigation of the facts in the case. This committee then reports its findings to the next annual meeting of the National Association. If the National Association concludes that the college or university has been guilty of a violation of its principles, it votes to place that institution upon its censured list. The effect of the action is simply a notice, or warning, to the entire educational profession that this particular institution is not in good standing with the Association. This action has two major effects in the profession: in the first place, members of the teaching profession are extremely hesitant to accept a position in this institution under these conditions. This makes it very difficult for the institution to recruit good faculty personnel. In addition, good faculty members in residence will often accept offers to other institutions rather than remain under these conditions. Thus, in both cases, placing of an institution upon the Association's censured list handicaps the institution severely in its competition to hold its own faculty, and to recruit new ones of comparable abilities. In other words, censuring strikes a serious blow to an institution's prestige.

Once an institution has been censured it remains in this status until the Association is convinced, by later investigations, that the conditions of its censureship have been satisfactorily corrected. In the case of The University of Texas, the censureship lasted for nine years.

The Association was in touch with us at the university almost from the beginning of our troubles, and kept in close touch with us during the entire period of the controversy. Dr. Ralph Himstead was at that time the Executive Director of the Association with his national headquarters in Washington, D. C. He made several special trips to the university during this period to consult with the faculty, administration, and Regents concerning the issues as they developed. He was thoroughly familiar with every detail of the controversy, and was a great help as mediator in helping us deal with the issues. His services were especially helpful during the Regents' efforts to abolish the tenure system and to destroy the principles of academic freedom. At one point, he made the statement that the situation at The University of Texas was the clearest case of the violation of academic freedom that the Association had ever been called upon to investigate.

The Association's report of its findings at The University of Texas was published in full in the Association's Bulletin for June 1946. That report was quite detailed in its analysis of the controversy, and it is much too long to be included in full here. However, a few selected quotations from the report will help the reader better to understand some of the basic issues of this controversy as seen from the point of view of this prestigious association.

Some of those statements concerning the controversy were as follows:

This situation . . . was precipitated by dismissals and threats of dismissals of members of the Faculty of The University of Texas by the institution's Board of Regents, contrary to the recommendations of the President, the Vice-President, the deans, and the department chairmen concerned, and by the subsequent summary dismissal of Dr. Homer P. Rainey from the presidency of the University. . . .

It was the hope of Committee A that the Board of Regents as thus reconstituted (after three had resigned) would undertake a judicious review of the facts of the total situation at the University. This the Board did not do. . . .

At this meeting [January 26, 1945—the first under the reconstituted Board] the Board was presented with many requests for the reinstatement of Dr. Rainey, among them one that had been authorized by an overwhelming majority of the Faculty of the University. These requests were ignored. . . .

In the opinion of Committee A, little in Mr. Woodward's statement [a four-hour speech at the first meeting of the new Board, January 26, 1945] was directed to the merits of the situation at The University of Texas. Most of the statement is irrelevant as regards the clarification of the facts with a view to reaching a just decision. . . .

With reference to the difficulties in the Medical School, the evidence indicates that it was not until Dr. Rainey had become *persona non grata* to certain members of the Board of Regents, because of his opposition to their attempts to repress freedom of teaching and research, that there were any manifestations of differences of opinion between him and the Board concerning the plans and policies for the Medical School. . . .

Committee A has given careful consideration to the testimony and other data relating to the difficulties in the Medical School of The University of Texas and finds nothing in the record which indicates that these difficulties motivated the decision of the Board of Regents to dismiss Dr. Rainey. The Committee believes that Dr. Rainey would have been dismissed even though there had been no difficulties in connection with the Medical School and that no useful purpose would be served by presenting a detailed report of the vicissitudes of the Medical School. . . .

In the opinion of Committee A Dr. Rainey was not dismissed because of mistakes in administration. . . . It is the considered judgment of Committee A that Dr. Rainey was dismissed because he refused to yield to pressure by the Board concerning teaching and research and, also, because of his philosophy of freedom in education. The Committee believes that if Dr. Rainey had not opposed the attempts at repression on the part of members of the Board, which included an attempt to destroy tenure at the University, his position as president would have remained secure, but that there would have been many dismissals from the faculty. . . .

Committee A is also of the opinion that these teachers would have been dismissed if Dr. Rainey had been a pliable president, and if the American Association of Universty Professors and other educational organizations had not intervened. . . .

The morale of the Faculty of The University of Texas during Dr. Rainey's administration was high, very high. . . .

Until it became evident that the Board of Regents was determined not to reinstate Dr. Rainey the Faculty was almost unanimous in seeking his reinstatement—no finer testimonial could be given any university president. . . .

Dr. Rainey believes in academic freedom. He believes that what constitutes a proper exercise of academic freedom is a matter for the determination of an institution's administrative officers and Faculty. Dr. Rainey also believes that the public has an interest in academic freedom and that without academic freedom an educational institution cannot fulfill its obligation to its students and to the public. Dr. Rainey's convictions in these matters are in accord with the philosophy of the American Association of University Professors. In the opinion of Committee A a university president who yields to pressure designed to weaken or destroy academic freedom is unfit to hold his significant position. The Committee believes, also, that a university president who resists efforts to weaken or destroy academic freedom and who seeks clarification of the issues involved in cases of attempts to repress freedom, with a view to bringing about adjustments in accordance with the principles of academic freedom generally observed by the administration of institutions of higher education, should have the gratitude and the support of the profession and of the public. For his efforts in behalf of academic freedom at The University of Texas, Dr. Rainey has earned the gratitude of our profession and the friends of education throughout the country. . . .

Apropos of this situation the Faculty of The University of Texas is to be commended for its courage and tenacity in opposing systematic, persistent, and continuous attempts by a politically dominant group to impose its social and educational views upon the Universiy.

As a result of the Committee's report the Council of the Association by a unanimous vote placed the administration of The University of Texas on the Association's list of censured administrations, where it remained for a period of nine years.

EPILOGUE   It would seem that a conflict which occurred a quarter of a century ago could have only limited relevance to the contemporary scene. And yet it is precisely because this is not the case that this book has been written.

The years following my association with The University of Texas have witnessed a growing concern over the administration of our colleges and universities, a concern which has been dramatized by recent developments and unrest in schools across the country. Unhappily, I must point to the fact that many of these issues of concern today were part of my conflict with the Regents of The University of Texas twenty-five years ago.

We are, today, faced with a national crisis in the administration of our universities! This crisis has many facets, some of the most important of which are: how shall our universities be governed? How shall the governing boards be chosen, and how extensive shall be their powers? What shall be the role and function of the administration, especially the president? The president has no legal power: legal power rests with the Board of Regents, which delegates powers to the president as it sees fit. The president can make no final decisions he can make only recommendations which are subject to approval or rejection by the Board.

The relationship of the president to the governing board and to the faculty and students has reached a critical stage. It is so critical that most presidents today are faced with an almost impossible situation: they have to be "crisis managers" without power and authority commensurate with their terrific responsibilities. A new definition of the president's power and authority can no longer be delayed without increasing this crisis. In fact, college administrators have recently organized their own national association; its purpose will be to "promote and perpetuate the profession of administration in higher education. It will attempt to define the rights and responsibilities of institutions and administrators, and to establish a recognized system of ethics and standards." (*The Chronicle of Higher Education*, October 19, 1970). The realization of these objectives will be instrumental in finding a solution to problems relating to the administration of higher education in the United States.

Another set of significant questions relates to the role and function of the faculty. Are the members of the faculty mere "employees," as advocated by Mr. Dudley Woodward in this report? The faculties have responded with a resounding "No!" Since 1915 they have organized and promoted their own organization, the American Association of University Professors (A.A.U.P.), through which they have enunciated some basic principles of the relationship between the faculty and the governing body. These principles have been widely accepted by every major educational body in the United States since 1940. The general acceptance of these principles, which deal primarily with academic freedom and tenure, has been one of the great stabilizing factors in the governing of colleges and universities for the last thirty years. No system of control for the future can succeed without due consideration of the role of the faculty.

More recently the student body has asserted in strong, positive terms its demands for a part in the control and administration of the universities. Students' demands cannot be overlooked in any future reorganization of our system of higher education. The A.A.U.P. has recognized the legitimacy of student demands, and has had a special committee drafting a set of basic principles relative to student participation in the administration of their universities. While a good start has been made in formulating the role of students, much more needs to be done.

Thus, the administration of higher education is in a crisis period. This will continue until all the groups involved, Regents, administrators, faculty and students, can, through a long process of negotiation, agree upon their respective roles. For the sake of the welfare of higher education these negotiations should go forward as rapidly as possible. I hope that this case study has thrown significant light upon these critical problems.

The Tower and the Dome $5.95

How shall a state supported university be
governed? How shall the governing boards
be chosen? What shall be the role and function of the university president and faculty;
indeed, of the university itself?

During his term as president of The University of Texas, from 1939-1944, Homer P.
Rainey waged a continuous battle with the
Board of Regents, over these, and other issues relating to the role of the university in
modern society.

The significance of these issues has not
diminished after the passage of a quarter of
a century. There is, in fact, a current national
crisis in the administration of our universities,
a crisis which makes the subject of this work
a timely and important contribution to the
field of higher education.

In *The Tower and the Dome*, the author, a
nationally known educator, presents his views
on these issues, together with the first full
and complete account of his unsuccessful five
year fight with the Regents for academic freedom and tenure at The University of Texas.
At that time, many editorials pointed out that
this was not simply a local affair, that it was
relevant to the entire field of higher education
in the United States, an observation which has
been amply supported by the many recent
developments in colleges and universities
across the country.

The Tower and the Dome is a book that will
be of interest to every American who is concerned with the present system of higher education in this country. It is a book that should
be read by every educator and elected official.